Ron Paul
REVOLUTION

History In the Making

by Mark Frazier

*Why freedom is the ultimate product for
Evangelism Marketing*

ISBN 978-0-6151-8775-4

First Published in United States of America 2008 by

MARK PROFFIT

406 W. High St. #1

Jackson, MI 49203

www.MarkProffitt.com

Table of Contents

Why Am I Writing This Book?

I love freedom, my country and my fellow man.

What's happening with the Ron Paul Presidential Campaign is changing the world and much of what is happening is not being recorded. More importantly only a few people have the background and involvement to know and understand this ground breaking story. My hope is to show what's happening, explain how it is happening and help the Revolution continue.

"We are running for president through Ron Paul."

Ron Paul is only the rallying point for the freedom movement. The Ron Paul Revolution isn't about a man its about an idea. When Ron Paul is asked how his campaign harnessed the Internet he accurately says, "We didn't harness the Internet, they harnessed us!"

Tens of thousands of people across the USA and all around the world are making a stand. They are making their voices heard. Each individual is singing the song of freedom in harmony with all the others. The tiniest voice, far removed from the centers of power, joins with others to become a huge chorus too loud to be ignored.

This movement is more than just American politics, its a global phenomenon made possible by recent advances in technology.

I've been working in the high tech world for over 20 years. From Apple to Microsoft, Nintendo to Hewlett Packard, and the United States Department of Justice to BitTorrent I've contributed much to the Information Age.

Additionally, I've been a volunteer to freedom oriented politics for 10 years. Having contacts across the board I easily moved within the various groups to experience things first hand that were hidden from most people. Without the learning curve of new comers to Ron Paul's message, I was able to understand the complex interaction of events as they occurred.

Finally my contacts in the media opened doors to help me get access to all sides of the political action. Being able to directly speak to the media I have a broader perspective that no one else seems to have.

My personal blog www.MarkProffitt.com discusses effects of the information age being felt all over the world. We are in the middle of a dramatic shift from an age of scarcity to abundance. Freedom is part of that shift. The institutions of the past are not equipped to deal with or even understand the new world. They see their existence threatened by the changes underway and are reacting violently to the shift.

I hope this book will help all people understand the changes underway and learn how to move through the turmoil and into a brighter future that is now possible.

Image 1: Ron Paul & Mark Frazier on Boat Ride to Mackinac Island

Mackinac Island Blow Back

Mackinac Island is a beautiful and unique place. To keep the special character of the place, no motorized vehicles are allowed on the island. The only modes of transport on the island are horse drawn carriages, bicycles or walking. Its like stepping back in time.

Other than by private plane or boat the only way on or off the island is via high speed ferry boat. The ferry boats run every half hour but when the last boat leaves at 9:30 pm you are stuck on the island until the morning.

I was in a unique situation for attending the Republican Leadership Conference on Mackinac Island. I was an independent producer submitting video to NBC and I was traveling with the Ron Paul supporters. My NBC press pass got me full access to the conference. Traveling with the Ron Paul supporters allowed me special access to events no one else saw.

After spending the entire day on the island covering events and filming video, I was heading back to the mainland to share a hotel room with Ron Paul supporters. As I walked up to the line of people waiting on the pier for the last ferry boat of the evening, I heard someone near the back of the line say "Look, there's Rudy Giuliani."

Rudy and about six people from his staff approached, I walked up to Giuliani, introduced myself and asked for an interview. As we were shaking hands, a few people at the back of the line nearby started chanting quietly "Ron Paul – Ron Paul".

Giuliani looked over my shoulder and his face went white as he started to realize the situation he was in. The entire line waiting for the boat, over 300 people, were all Ron Paul supporters. The experience was surreal.

During the first 2008 Republican Presidential Debate Rudy Giuliani tried to capitalize on being the mayor of New York during the 9/11 Attacks by taking a cheap shot at Ron Paul. Giuliani interrupted and misquoted Ron Paul to ridicule what was never said.

Ron Paul said, "They don't come over here to attack us because we are rich and free. They come over here because we've been over there."

The moderator shot back asking, "Are you suggesting we deserved to be attacked?"

Ron Paul responded, "No! I'm suggesting we should listen to what the people that attacked us say were the reasons they attacked us."

Giuliani cut in saying, "I've never heard something so absurd as we deserved to be attacked."

Ron Paul took the high ground, as he always does, and restated what he said and quoted the official 9/11 Report from the CIA substantiating what he had actually said. Giuliani sneered and continued with insults. He even demanded an apology. Giuliani thought he had scored points with his condescending lie.

Now Giuliani was face to face with his worst nightmare.

Nobody could believe this was happening. I'm sure a few of the people in that crowd at least thought to themselves, "I would love to catch the pompous jerk in a dark alley." And now they had.

They all started quietly chanting "Ron Paul, Ron Paul". Giuliani shrank and looked like he was going to be sick. He quickly walked to the front of the line as I followed close behind. The entire time the chanting grew louder and more cheerful. His staff was looking frantic. When the boat arrived, one of the crew asked the Ron Paul supporters to stay on the dock while Giuliani and staff boarded the boat first and sat up front. Giuliani hid in the bridge with the captain, not to be seen again until the end of the trip.

The Ron Paul supporters were laughing and chanting. They all sat in their seats right behind Giuliani's staff and politely but very loudly chanted support for Ron Paul, all the way across the straights of Mackinac. A few yelled, "Did you read the 9/11 Report yet?" Which stated the facts Giuliani said he never heard.

I was sitting right behind the Giuliani staff with the camera crew from ABC. The guys from ABC were ecstatic, this was a great story and they were the only ones that would get it. You can see me behind the reporters as they pan the camera.

Even though the video was captured by ABC and what happened was clearly evident other media spun this as Ron Paul supporters being out of control and crazy.

Remember that Giuliani had to walk past the line on the dock. At no time did anyone do anything but make noise.

Citizen journalism helped set the facts straight. The ABC camera only got one angle of the event. But two other amateur cameras also caught the event and clearly showed how many people were there and that they were all sitting in their seats.

The negative interpretation was a bit of a shock to the people that had been there. The Ron Paul supporters were so wrapped up in being discounted and ridiculed they didn't grasp what was really happening. This would be an important lesson for that bunch of Ron Paul supporters. They failed to notice they were absolutely the majority. They out numbered any of the other candidates supporters even though college kids were hired by the other candidates to wear t-shirts and hand out materials. When the media reported on the event, the Ron Paul supporters learned it's very important to watch what you do so that people will perceive you properly.

Being #1 was something to which they needed to become accustomed.

Image 2: ABC News Cover Rudy Giuliani on Mackinac Ferry With Ron Paul Supporters
http://www.youtube.com/watch?v=0mrbZ6cnZKk

More Money from Soldiers than any other GOP Candidate

http://www.youtube.com/watch?v=an2i0t2o5rw

Many people claim we must support our troops by not speaking out against the war. The troops think differently. They support the only candidate who will end the war and would have prevented it in the first place.

Image 3: Ron Paul vs. Giuliani @ South Carolina Debate
http://www.youtube.com/watch?v=AD7dnFDdwu0

Who Is Ron Paul?

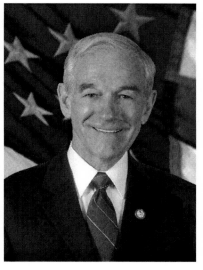

Ron Paul sprang from relative obscurity to regularly breaking records for presidential campaigns. He's everywhere on the Internet. Signs and bumper stickers cover the country. The establishment is shocked and doesn't understand what is happening. When asked how his campaign harnessed the Internet to generate more grass roots support than all the other candidates combined, he says, "We didn't, the grass roots harnessed us."

Ron Paul is the most unlikely person to be a star. He is totally unassuming, always approachable and polite. He truly is the wise old country doctor who always has time for his patients.

During 30 years of public service he's become known as the iconoclastic United States Congressman that always stands to defend the Constitution and oppose taxes. His perfect voting record earned him the nick name Dr. No for being so honest and principled. The lobbyists don't even bother trying to influence him. Ron Paul can't be bought.

Before 2007, he wasn't a household name by any means but people who knew him loved him. When he announced he was running for President in the 2008 election, people like me were both surprised and excited.

The best you can say of most candidates is they're the lesser of two evils. People knowledgeable in economics and politics often joked they would vote for Ron Paul if he ran. No one ever expected him to run; it was just wishful thinking. And now there he is, seeking the Republican Party nomination. WOW!

When I heard Ron Paul was running I immediately dropped everything I was doing and got involved with other supporters that were working to make the Ron Paul Revolution reality. I knew that my background and expertise at Evangelism Marketing could be extremely beneficial to this type of political campaign.

Obviously, I'm not the only person dedicating their time and money to support Ron Paul. Some people have special skills and others are just normal people that respect the man and love the message. He is the right man at the right time catalyzing what has become an international freedom movement.

Born in 1935 in Green Tree, Pennsylvania, Ron Paul lived through massive changes in the world. He grew up on a farm during the Great Depression a son of German Immigrants. He lived through World War II, the Cold War, Civil Rights, Sexual Revolution, Golden Age of Television, and the birth and growth of personal computers and the Internet.

After completing his medical degree at Duke he began medical residency at Henry Ford Hospital in Detroit, Michigan. His training was interrupted in 1963 when he enlisted into the U.S. Air Force during the Cuban Missile Crisis or face being drafted. He remained in the military during the early years of the Vietnam War treating pilots in South Korea, Iran, Ethiopia, and Turkey, but was never sent to Vietnam. The experience of performing physicals on helicopter pilot candidates, at a time when he saw many

Image 4: Ron Paul Air Force Photograph

helicopters being shot down, deeply affected Paul. His indirect association with the Vietnam War catalyzed his rejection of isolationist foreign policies and military intervention.

He saw an important reason to peacefully interact with other nations and the need to avoid interfering in the internal affairs of other nations, especially militarily.

Dr. Paul honorably served his nation as a captain in the Air Force and continued in the Air National Guard while completing a residency in obstetrics and gynecology.

He moved to Surfside Beach, Texas and went into private practice as an obstetrician delivering over 4,000 babies during his career.

Ron Paul is a family man who has remained faithfully married to his wife Carol for over 50 years while fathering 5 children, 18 grand children, and one great grand child.

Integrity is the word that best describes Ron Paul. He objects to Medicaid

& Medicare because the government uses force to take from one person to give to another. His objection isn't just philosophical; he puts his money where his mouth is, literally. Rather than take Medicaid or Medicare, if a patient could not afford to pay, he would treat them at a discount or for free. Keeping with that principle of not taking from others, he did not allow his children to accept government loans to go to college.

He often talks about working nights in a church hospital for $3 per hour to earn extra money. He points out that before the government got involved in health care, charitable hospitals never asked for insurance and never turned anyone away. He points out that technology has driven the prices of other things down, but the prices of medical care have skyrocketed. He's personally experienced the red tape involved with being a doctor and how its driving doctors away from practicing medicine. The lack of medical doctors is causing shortages that further increase costs to consumers.

His favorite activity is riding his bicycle. He is in better shape than many people in their 20's. If you walk with him be prepared to keep up. He is full of energy. You will be the one trying to keep up with him.

As a United States Congressman he is entitled to a very lucrative pension. He's declined that pension as well as returning a portion of his congressional budget every year. He is a man of his word preferring to lead by example.

Medicine isn't the only subject he intimately knows. He's extensively studied economics and public policy having published 6 books on the topics. He has served on both the House Sub-committee on Banking & Finance and the House Sub-committee on Foreign Relations during his 20 years in Congress.

His knowledge isn't just theoretical, he's lived through events that proved what he says is true. Repeatedly he's warned of the negative consequences of many of the government's actions and has had his predictions validated.

While commenting on the loss of freedom that has occurred in the United States, the head of public communications at Google who was interviewing him asked, "Is there any other country you think is more free than the United States?"

Dr. Paul responded, "Unfortunately more and more...Switzerland is a good example. I wouldn't mind being president of Switzerland. Do you know who the president of Switzerland is? Nobody does and I think that is pretty neat."

That says a lot about Ron Paul. He's not in politics for fame or fortune. He would rather ride his bicycle and be a grandfather. He's running for President of the United States because he cares about the country and feels obligated to do something about it. He's perhaps the last of a dying breed. He's not a politician, he is a statesman.

Join Us.

Thousands already have — throughout this nation and around the world. More men and women serving overseas have donated to this campaign than any other. Don't believe the cynical lie that we can't fight the big money that funds politics as usual. People of every age, race, and background, united by a message of freedom, peace, and prosperity, stand poised to take this country back.

Dr. Ron Paul

Lobbyists don't bother to visit him in Congress. Why? Because he never supports any bill that violates the Constitution or gives handouts to their bosses, no matter who they are. Ron Paul served his country as a flight surgeon. He was a popular physician who treated all in need whether they could pay or not. He is a devoted husband, father, and grandfather. He grows organic tomatoes and loves the land.

Ron Paul has been called the modern Thomas Jefferson. He is seeking to join you in a second American revolution to restore our liberty.

Authorized and paid for by Ron Paul 2008 PCC

Image 5: Improved Slim Jim

HOPE FOR AMERICA

Congressman Ron Paul is unique. He has a principled, consistent voting record that is not dictated by special interests in Washington, DC. Many promise in the election season; Ron Paul has always delivered. He has stood resolute against our government's interference overseas, in the economy, and in our personal lives. He is the champion of the Constitution.

Ron Paul will:

Bring the troops home, *now.*

Stop the looting of Social Security.

Save $1 trillion overseas, reducing our debt, helping veterans, children, and seniors, and cutting taxes.

End forced health screening and vaccinations.

Oppose WTO, NAFTA, CAFTA, and the NAU.

Fight for freedom to choose health care.

Stop corporate welfare and polluters.

Protect our privacy and civil liberties.

Stop the national ID card.

Oppose internet taxes and regulation.

www.RonPaul2008.com

State of Affairs

In 2007, President George W. Bush's approval rating is under 30%. The Democratic congress is ranked even lower. The Democrats won a lot of seats in congress in 2004 because they promised to change the direction the Republicans had taken with the war. Instead of changing direction they approved sending more troops into Iraq and reauthorized the draconian USA PATRIOT Act (Uniting and Strengthening America by Providing Appropriate Tools Required to Intercept and Obstruct Terrorism Act).

More U.S. Citizens have died because of invading Iraq than in the destruction of the World Trade Center on 9/11/2001 that sparked all of the recent military action in the Middle East. The government has spent nearly a trillion dollars on the war with money borrowed from China.

People are losing their houses with record setting foreclosure rates. The Federal Reserve doubled and maybe even tripled the money supply during the last 7 years causing prices of everything to go through the roof. There is no way to know how much money was created out of thin air because they stopped publishing reports in 2006. While the government reports we have low inflation and low unemployment the truth is evident on the street.

The US dollar is now worth less than the Canadian dollar, which had been the brunt of jokes for not being as valuable as the greenback.

Great Britain, France and Canada are rationing access to their supposedly free national health care because they are facing bankruptcy. And politicians promise to give the U.S. the same systems while millions of illegal aliens pour across the border to use all those "free" services while sending much of the money they earn home to their native countries.

People are frustrated with candidates whose policies are virtually indistinguishable from those of all the other candidates and disgusted with the broken promises, half truths and outright lies.

Business as usual isn't going to cut it anymore.

This is the first presidential election where nearly everyone has cell phones and Internet access. Citizen journalists are able to report the uncensored truth on their blogs and through videos on YouTube.

In 2004, 160 million cell phones were in use in the USA.

All this new communication technology makes spreading a message fast, simple and cheap.

Instead of grumbling to their friends, people tell the entire world exactly what they think and exactly what's happening in their town. Businesses have been using these innovations to achieve greater success more quickly than ever before.

The politician that taps into what is happening can change the world and its a good thing because it doesn't look like the world can survive more of the same.

Ron Paul comes to the scene with a very different message, very different approach and a track record of telling the truth and keeping his word. These are the exact right ingredients for success today.

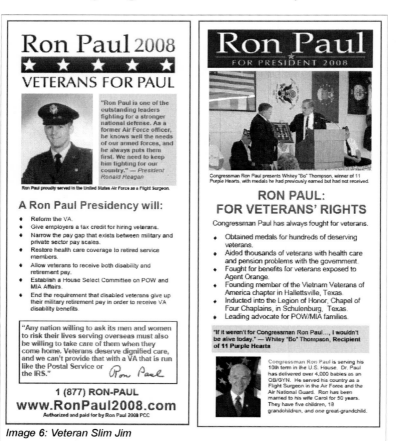

Image 6: Veteran Slim Jim

Start a Revolution

I learned Ron Paul was running for president the same way a lot of people did: from a home-made sign with a striking graphic hung from a freeway over pass.

I had followed Ron Paul for many years. When I first saw the sign, I didn't catch that it said Ron Paul. The "Love" portion of revolution is what I saw. It was the second time I saw the sign that I realized it said Ron Paul. I was surprised. Since it was in a college town I thought it might be the name

Image 7: Ron Paul Revolution - Phoenix, AZ
http://www.youtube.com/watch?v=Sw RXp8ZMdNQ

of a band. The first chance I got I typed Ron Paul Revolution into Google and learned he was running for president. Amazing!

I clicked through a couple links and found the www.RonPaulRevolution.com web site. The logo was the creation of Ernest Hancock. He and a friend at www.rescue-us.org started the whole thing. They created the first Meetup group in Phoenix, AZ and the message had already spread to Michigan.

In the beginning no one had campaign materials so people made their own and hit the road running. That kind of entrepreneurial spirit runs all through the Ron Paul campaign. But something more than entrepreneurial spirit was at play. The guys that made the logo also published templates and instructions for how to make your own signs and a cool music video showing his friends hanging the signs up. This direct form of donating time and creativity completely sidestepped issues of money. I'm not even sure there was an easy way to contribute money to the Ron Paul Presidential Campaign in the beginning.

By publishing the templates and instructions they were leaders. There wasn't any formal process. No one had to grant them authority. They did something productive and shared it with others. They led and others followed. Here is the link. You decide if you want to do what they did. http://www.rescue-us.org/new/RPR-HowTo

The official campaign still hasn't figured out how to organize and mobilize the supporters. The official campaign has unwittingly undermined the success of Ron Paul at every step. But Ron Paul supporters were used to dealing with out of touch centralized bureaucracies. The supporters responded to the official campaign exactly the way they treated government when it failed to live up to its promises, they went around it.

Routing around obstacles is a key characteristic of a distributed system. Its the same way the Internet works. Its how water flows. Distributed systems are the most resilient and usually find the most efficient solution.

Ron Paul Revolution signs were now out in the marketplace of ideas. The creators offered other Ron Paul supporters the choice to do what they did. If they liked what they saw they followed. If not, they were free to do something else or nothing at all. This was the purest example of the free market Ron Paul promotes.

Other people created signs asking, "Who is Ron Paul?" and "Google Ron Paul." The "who is" signs were popular for a while, but as more people became aware of Ron Paul and other signs with new slogans circulated the "Who Is" sign lost popularity. No one needed to tell the supporters what to do, they communicated amongst themselves and did what they felt was best for their own situation. This didn't always produce the best initial results but allowed the freedom to create some remarkable ideas. Real free market competition allowed the best ideas to flourish.

While the other candidates were meeting with deep pocketed contributors to solicit enough money to get started, Ron Paul's message was already reaching potential voters and supporters.

The signs weren't the only things they made. Using a website called CafePress.com they had t-shirts, bumper stickers, buttons and an entire range of products promoting the Ron Paul Revolution and people anywhere in the world could buy these items.

Users of CafePress upload their designs and select which items they would like to have imprinted and sold. CafePress handles the rest, making the items on demand, providing an online store, shipping the products when sold and automatically depositing profits in the designers' bank account.

The design of the "Ron Paul Revolution" logo wasn't the only one with Ron Paul designs for sale on CafePress. Hundreds of other items were also available. The official Ron Paul campaign had nothing to do with any of it and all this activity went on below the radar of the mainstream media. The disconnect from what was really happening would impact the campaign in many ways. Remedying part of the disconnect would be one of the ways I personally contributed to the revolution.

I talked with people in the media and found out what they thought about Ron Paul and his supporters. I discovered that they were generally receptive to Ron Paul's message but were put off by the way some of his supporters acted. The people who had been fighting in the freedom movement for a long time often were irritated that important issues were not covered by the large corporate media. And often the reason these people got involved in the first place was because of a negative event that personally affected them. Many had spent years researching issues in great detail. So naturally a lot of what they would say was new to the listener. If the new information conflicted with previously held believes there was resistance and misunderstandings. Those long time supporters had the incorrect belief that all the media was against them and Ron Paul. The supporters were correct that there were restrictions but some of it wasn't what they thought and there were ways to get around it.

People in the media, especially TV are accustomed to being treated with a lot of respect. Maybe they are treated with more respect than they even deserve. When I walked up to Rudolph Giuliani he was extremely polite to me. I knew that was because of the NBC press badge I was wearing. And I received the same treatment from Mitt Romney's staff when I spoke to them.

Treating everyone as an individual is a core value of Ron Paul and his supporters. The special treatment the media expects comes across to some of the grassroots supporters as condescending. And the media views some of the grassroots as aggressive.

In one case I sat down a group of about 50 Ron Paul supporters and told them the things the people in the media were saying about them. I explained that the media wanted to talk to Ron Paul supporters but the way the supporters were acting made it impossible to be able to do it.

Beyond the respect the TV media was accustomed to receiving they had technical limits on what they could show. Having a short sound bite that their viewers could easily relate to made it much easier for reporters to include a message in a story. And making it personal helped as well. TV makes its money from advertising so they aren't going to give free advertising to anyone unless it somehow benefits viewers and improves ratings.

The supporters I talked to were very surprised by what I told them but understood and began working the new information in to what they did.

Supporters complained about the official campaign material. The "slim jim" looked like any other political leaflet and had a 30 year old photo of Ron Paul with Ronald Reagan.

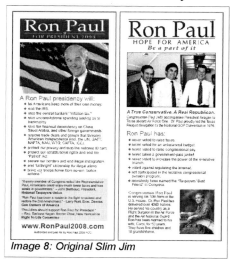
Image 8: Original Slim Jim

Ron Paul's message doesn't match typical catch phrases. The bullet items on the leaflet seemed disjointed and without further explanation would often turn people off.

The only thing that saved Ron Paul were his exceptionally well informed and dedicated supporters taking time to explain the positions and provide ways for people to find better information.

One example is Dr. Paul's stand on abortion. As an obstetrician he swore an oath to do no harm; so, he is strongly anti-abortion. He points out that as a doctor if he does something to harm an unborn child, even unintentionally, he can be held liable for his actions. On the other hand, its perfectly legal if the mother pays him to kill the baby in the womb.

Even though Ron Paul is strongly against abortion he keeps his commitment to uphold the Constitution and categorically declares the federal government has no authority in the matter. The constitutional position is abortion is a matter that must be left up to the individual states.

Following the Constitution relieves most of the objections on both sides of the issue. With 50 states each having laws reflecting the attitudes of its citizens its more likely to be legal somewhere than with a one size fits all ruling.

You can see with this issue that Dr. Paul's position isn't accurately represented by either "pro-choice" or "pro-life" authoritarian type of viewpoints.

Another issue many people try to oversimplify is the war in Iraq. Most of the other candidate's and their advocates in the media say if you oppose the war you don't want to defend the nation. They claim Ron Paul is an isolationist. The exact opposite of the truth. The soldiers understand the truth.

First, Ron Paul said to his colleagues in Congress before the invasion of Iraq, "If you want to go to war then declare war, fight it, win it and come home; but, don't get into unending police actions or nation building." Ron Paul went so far as to write up Articles of War for the others to sign. They refused to use the Constitutionally authorized method to grant the president approval to invade another nation. They broke the law.

When it was clear that the attacks of 9/11/2001 were not the result of another nation but were the actions of a small group of international criminals, Ron Paul recommended the Constitutionally authorized method for dealing with international criminals. He recommended, and still does recommend the method that worked in the past when the United States was being menaced by pirates off the east coast.

Letters of Marque and Reprisal function very much like a bounty on the heads of international criminals. Quickly after the United States issued Letters of Marque and Reprisal against the pirates terrorizing citizens along the east coast, the pirates were captured or killed and the terrorism stopped. Using the correct amount of force limits the risk to US soldiers and other innocent people. By following the Constitution we could have reversed the threat of terrorism instead of motivating a new generation seeking revenge.

Because many people knew nothing about Congressman Paul, they needed more information when they were exposed to his views for the first time. They also needed an easy way to come up to speed quickly.

Supporters created videos detailing his positions, quoting things he said and featuring news clips backing his statements. The videos created by supporters filled the gap in the campaign materials both exposing new people to his positions and educating supporters on how to express those positions in the most effective manner.

As more and more of these videos filled YouTube, people began making DVD collections to hand out. One supporter created a web site to supply low cost copies of a DVD he compiled. www.ronpauldvd.com. The first primary is only weeks away and the official campaign still hasn't made their own DVD. It wasn't until months into the campaign that they even started making position statement videos. Even though the videos are online they are not included on the issues pages of the same topic. And 10 months after announcing his candidacy there still isn't a broadcast quality collection of videos.

Its a shame the official campaign hasn't published a DVD because it would be the most effective tool for winning new supporters. The interview of Ron Paul @ Google is the closest thing available.

Dr. Paul's
Record on Health Care

The federal government has turned a free market health care system that was once the envy of the world into a federally-managed disaster. Few people realize that Congress forced the HMO system on us.

As a doctor, Ron Paul knows our health care system needs real change. Patients and doctors should be in charge - not corporate America, not the HMOs, not the big drug companies, and not government bureaucrats.

Government health care only means long waiting periods, lack of choice, poor care, and frustration. Many Canadians, fed up with socialized medicine, come to the U.S. in order to obtain care. Socialized medicine will not magically work here.

It is time to take back our health care!

Dr. Paul supports:

- Making all medical expenses tax deductible.
- Eliminating federal regulations that discourage small businesses from providing coverage.
- Allowing you to use supplements and vitamins to stay healthy.
- Giving doctors the freedom to collectively negotiate with insurance companies and drive down the cost of medical care.
- Allowing patients to buy cheaper prescription drugs from other countries.

www.RonPaul2008.com

Authorized and paid for by Ron Paul 2008 PCC.

Ron Paul 2008
FOR HEALTH FREEDOM

Dr. Ron Paul

- **Opposes the FDA's move for greater control over nutrients and vitamins,** and the directives of the UN's World Food Code (CODEX).

-**Authored the Health Freedom Protection Act,** HR 2117, to ensure Americans have access to uncensored information about supplements and natural remedies.

- **Supports the Access to Medical Treatment Act,** H.R. 2717, which expands the ability of Americans to use alternative medicine and new treatments.

- **Opposes forced vaccinations and mental screenings of American citizens.**

Congressman Ron Paul is serving his 10th term in the U.S. House. Dr. Paul has delivered over 4,000 babies as an OB/GYN. He served his country as a Flight Surgeon in the Air Force and the Air National Guard. Ron has been married to his wife, Carol, for 50 years. They have five children, 18 grandchildren, and one great-grandchild.

"We must stop federal government interference with our freedom to choose what we eat and how we take care of our health." - Dr. Ron Paul

Image 9: Health Care Slim Jim

Seeing Is Believing

Ron Paul is sincere and speaks the truth. He's not smooth and isn't polished. But he can answer any question with facts and well thought out understanding. He doesn't talk in sound bites or try to emotionally manipulate people. In a traditional advertising based campaign that is a huge disadvantage. In an Evangelism Marketing campaign its great. All it takes is for people to hear Ron Paul explain his whole message and they become fans. That is exactly what the video of Ron Paul @ Google did.

One of my friends was a hard core Neocon. She voted for G.W. Bush, supported the war on terrorism and even went so far as saying she wanted to have Sean Hannity's baby. It took a while for me to talk her into just watching Ron Paul @ Google. When she finally watch the video a miracle occurred. She went from being Sean Hannity's biggest fan to finding her candidate. Now she will vote for Ron Paul.

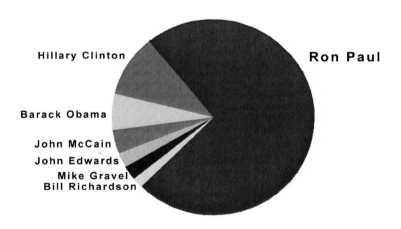

Image 10: Percentage Views of Video of Candidates @ Google

The video of Ron Paul @ Google is one of the most popular among Ron Paul supporters because of its effectiveness. Hillary Clinton's interview at Google was published February 25, 2007 and only has 56,251 views. Ron Paul's interview was published July 14, 2007 and has 404,574 views, 2.7

times as many as all the other candidates combined.

Candidates @ Google Videos as of December 10, 2007

Candidate	Party	Date	Views	% Views	Views / Day
Ron Paul	Republican	07/14/07	405,823	73.5%	2,723.6
Hillary Clinton	Democrat	02/25/07	56,251	10.2%	195.3
Barack Obama	Democrat	11/14/07	33,670	6.1%	1,295.0
John McCain	Republican	05/04/07	21,498	3.9%	97.7
John Edwards	Democrat	05/30/07	13,786	2.5%	71.1
Mike Gravel	Democrat	10/11/07	12,556	2.3%	209.3
Bill Richardson	Republican	05/15/07	8,521	1.5%	40.8
			552,105	100.00%	

Table 1: Views of Candidates @ Google Videos

Anyone with a computer and a high speed Internet connection can watch the video of Ron Paul @ Google. In fact I wasn't actually talking to my friend, I was sending her messages through online instant chat. I sent her the link. She clicked on it and instantly began watching the video. If we had talked in another environment I might never have been able to get her to watch the video. It was easy and I caught her when she was receptive.

Watching a video while she was on her computer was easy and free. She could stop any time she wanted so there was zero commitment. This is an essential element of Evangelism Marketing. Let people try it. If your message really is good they will fall in love and become a new evangelist.

Love breeds freedom, and freedom breeds love.

Whether intentionally or just because of who he is, Ron Paul doesn't use short catchy phrases. This hurts him in the broadcast media because they are always looking for the 5 second sound bite.

One of the reasons TV news looks for the sound bite is they have limited air time. Additionally, through decades of conditioning, viewers attention spans are very short and the increased number of choices overloads people with things fighting for their attention. The Internet provides even more things vying for your attention, but makes it possible to focus on what you want when you want. This solves the attention problem.

Additionally, when a friend recommends an item, they understand what is meaningful to you. This helps you find relevant media you are more likely to want to watch. Your friend might have even summarized it for you making it easier for you to digest.

TV, radio and even newspapers have a short time to catch attention. When something is published on the Internet, it's possible for it to reach audiences that didn't have a chance to catch it the first time. This allows a wider range of people to see things and for them to dig deeper into subjects they find interesting.

People have been talking about issues like alternative health care, homeschooling, asset forfeiture, national sovereignty, currency debasement, the second amendment, and censorship for a very long time. This huge collection of articles and videos published over many years are now being discovered by people that never could had found them before. Even books published hundreds of years ago are available on the Internet. This lets people quickly see connections between events and issues.

The Internet allows old news to find new interest. A video or article published years ago can now get worldwide attention. Copies of things thought to be lost down the memory hole reappear and spread. This helps Ron Paul whose consistently said the same things and voted the same way for 30 years. Other politicians hate the Internet because the truth is devastating when you change with the wind or your conduct is, if not criminal, very unflattering.

Politicians have traditionally relied on spin doctors to influence perceptions of fact and often manipulate the facts to fit their goals. When the news outlets are limited spin doctors can be very powerful. But in the world of the Internet people can speak back. They can expose lies and make sure the truth is available for everyone that wants to see and hear.

Image 11: Semi trailer Ron Paul sign

Image 12: Ron Paul @ Google

More Than Politics

The Ron Paul Revolution as its come to be called is much more than politics. Ron Paul's message is freedom. Not just empty words but real freedom. Freedom to run your own life. Freedom to make your own mistakes and freedom to enjoy your rewards.

Is such a radical idea of being responsible for yourself feasible? It's been so long since there were physical frontiers in the United States that no one remembers what it's really like to make it on your own. The only argument against freedom is fear.

What happens when people are allowed to decide for themselves? What do they do with their money, time, and with each other?

The spontaneous grassroots movement shows us exactly what people will do when they are free.

Ron Paul supporters create their own marketing materials, manufacture & distribute products of all kinds, form groups to fund and share work to complete large projects.

Technology makes all this possible but it was freedom that made the technology possible. While big businesses cozy up to government for legislation to stop competition and easy money from fat contracts, high tech entrepreneurs and hobbyists are busy innovating.

Cell phones, personal computers, digital video cameras, and websites offering every service imaginable at prices only possible in a truly free market, made it easy for supporters of Ron Paul to do anything they needed to promote their favorite presidential candidate.

Ron Paul has a lot of support from the high tech "geeks" who are revolutionizing the world. They are educated and understand the issues and aren't impressed by slick presentation. They know how to find the truth and demand truth from anyone talking to them, especially a politician.

When geeks discover something isn't possible they make it possible. They form virtual companies over night while discussing issues ranging from foreign policy, macro economics, and the latest discovery in molecular biology, to ancient history.

Geeks are in constant communication using every imaginable technology including e-mail, blogs, cell phones, SMS, voice over Internet protocol (VOIP) telephony like Skype, instant messaging, forums, and chat rooms. The chat rooms and forums in particular are breeding grounds for everything that leads to taking action.

Dozens to hundreds of people discuss and debate topics, all at the same time. They learn to express themselves quickly and convincingly. If someone makes a claim someone else will quickly post a link, either confirming or debunking the claim. Chat room participants become highly skilled at thinking on their feet and defending their thoughts.

When someone has a good idea others chime in and the discussion immediately turns to making it happen. The people most interested join a private chat and work out the details. Basically forming a "virtual company" or organization on the spot.

Geeks use Open Source tools to quickly get projects running. The Open Source community drives the Internet. All the significant parts of the Internet are created in the Open Source community, from web browsers, to e-mail, to chat, to VOIP. The Open Source community is comfortable with sharing to achieve goals.

> Open Source is the practice of allowing users to modify and customize a product. Often improvements are then shared with others. Most Open Source products are free for personal use.

Many of the best tools in the world are free. I'm writing this book using Open Office and edited the images using Gimp, both free open source tools.

People contribute their time to improve these tools because they use the tools. This is not charity. Its a non-cash co-op. The value of having the tools to use is enough reward to motivate highly skilled people to build and then share the best products in the market.

The the cooperative nature itself, plus the increased productivity of the tools created makes things possible that were simply too expensive or specialized to find in the for profit world.

Ron Paul supporters want him elected. They don't need to be paid. They view the increased freedom that comes from Ron Paul being president as the reward for all the hard work. And because freedom is the only profit, they can do things for less cost than possible using professional campaigners. This opens up options that wouldn't even be possible in the strictly for profit world.

If a project does need money they instantly begin fund raising by using tools like ChipIn.com. People all over the world contribute to projects they support. This direct fund raising resonates very well with Ron Paul's message of individual freedom and responsibility. Ron Paul supporters are proving we don't need taxes or centralized bureaucracies for everyone to have what they need.

Image 13: ChipIn Fund Raising Widget

Geeks have been quietly doing things this way for decades. For geeks in Silicon Valley, their favorite sport is becoming a billionaire and making all their employees rich. Tools are now so wide spread and easy to use, everyone can participate in that type of free market innovation.

Powered by a totally new type of marketing called Evangelism Marketing, the geeks changed the world. Using the same techniques, geeks and other Ron Paul supporters, are changing the world in a different way.

Ron Paul is promoting ideas and the information age is in full swing promoting Ron Paul.

Open Source Initiative – OSI

http://www.opensource.org/

The Open Source Initiative (OSI) is a non-profit corporation formed to educate about and advocate for the benefits of open source and to build bridges among different constituencies in the open-source community.

Open source is a development method for software that harnesses the power of distributed peer review and transparency of process. The promise of open source is better quality, higher reliability, more flexibility, lower cost, and an end to predatory vendor lock-in.

Many of the concepts proven in the open-source community work well in a government of the people, by the people and for the people.

Creative Commons

http://creativecommons.org/

Creative Commons provides free tools that let authors, scientists, artists, and educators easily mark their creative work with the freedoms they want it to carry. You can use CC to change your copyright terms from "All Rights Reserved" to "Some Rights Reserved."

Creative Commons overcomes the recent laws that drastically reduce the ability of information to be shared.

What is Evangelism Marketing?

Evangelism Marketing is the process of
making customers so happy
they freely sell your product for you.

Traditional advertising based marketing depends on interrupting potential customers and using psychological tactics to get them to buy your product. Its manipulative, annoying and often down right dishonest. And the worst abusers are political campaigns.

Traditional advertising requires lots of money to bombard people. On average it takes six exposures to a brand just to get people to remember the name.

Evangelism Marketing costs less and is more effective than traditional advertising based marketing. After years of being lied to and annoyed by interruptions people get very good at ignoring and even avoiding advertising.

The fundamental rule of Evangelism Marketing is <u>Tell the Truth</u>. Word of mouth is at the heart of Evangelism Marketing and it depends on the truth. You don't have to sell the truth, just share it and people are glad they got the information.

No one wants to risk ruining their reputation with their friends and family for free. And everyone immediately gets that creepy feeling the second someone starts pitching a multi-level marketing scam.

When you have a great experience you tell your friends and they are grateful. If their experience is also great, they become an evangelist as well. When a customer is unhappy, look out! Unhappy customers quickly tell everyone they know. Word of Mouth is the most powerful form of marketing.

The official Ron Paul campaign didn't know anything about Evangelism Marketing and barely comprehends the Internet. I can point out dozens of ways the Ron Paul campaign could make their campaign more effective. But one of the miracles of Evangelism Marketing is customers are spreading the message so they are free to improve on the methods used.

The Ron Paul campaign staff aren't responsible for the success. In fact the success is despite all of their well meaning but destructive moves.

One of my biggest challenges as a volunteer was performing the tasks to guide the Evangelism Marketing without the benefit of support from the official campaign. The campaign could have achieve twice the results in half the time if myself or someone else with Evangelism Marketing experience was receiving cooperation from the official Ron Paul campaign.

Measuring results was a big challenge. Since I didn't have access to the official campaign web statistics, campaign finance data or telephone logs I was operating blindly.

The live contribution meter was one of the items I requested they provide. Not only has it helped the grassroots see progress, it encourages participation by giving instant recognition.

Even if I did have access to the www.RonPaul2008.com logs, visits to the website don't tell the whole story. If this was an Evangelism Marketing campaign for a product that is sold, you would measure success by sales and profits. This is an election. The only real measure doesn't come until after all your efforts are finished. Campaign contributions, web site visits, polls and everything else are only proxies for future votes.

Since most of the activity of Evangelism Marketing is happening outside your control, you need ways to measure the outside activity. I use a collection of publicly available sources. Two of the sources I use most are Google Trends and Alexa.com.

Google Trends allows you to see the relative popularity of a search term and the number of news articles published.

This is extremely powerful since Google tracks every search performed. Google is effectively conducting continuous polling of 263 million people without any bias. Because Google Trends watches what people actually search for, it's a much more accurate measure than polling.

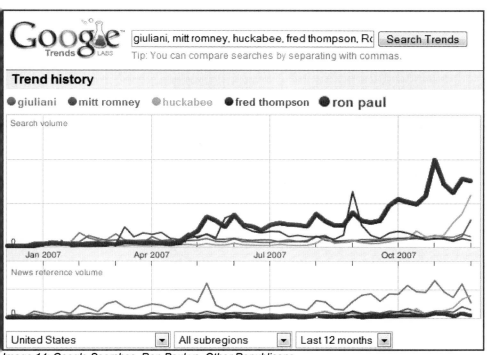

Image 14: Google Searches, Ron Paul vs. Other Republicans

The bottom graph shows the number of news articles matching the search term. Notice the correlation of searches to news articles for the other candidates. Ron Paul has almost no news coverage as compared to the other candidates. Searches for Ron Paul are increasing without support from the news. People are finding out about him other ways and then searching for more information. Search results that do not depend on news coverage or advertising is a clear sign your message appeals to people.

Looking at the long term graph, you can see Ron Paul's search results are growing exponentially.

Millions of searches are occurring and those people are finding out about Ron Paul somehow. Look at the large spike after November 5th, 2007. The news coverage from the Money Bomb caused a huge surge. It's very

Image 15: Long Term Ron Paul Google Trends

important to see the searches didn't drop back to pre-Money Bomb levels. Search growth continued at the high exponential growth rate.

Exponential growth is a sign of natural growth. As people discover Ron Paul they tell other people which leads to more and more searches. Ron Paul's support is growing naturally. This exponential trend also means the number of people finding out about him will grow increasingly quickly. The more people find out about Ron Paul the more people are telling others about Ron Paul.

Giuliani has 10 times as many news articles about him as does Ron Paul. Even though the media is pushing Giuliani, searches for him are steadily dropping. Regular people are not promoting Giuliani. Any support Giuliani might have is a media creation. On his own he could not maintain interest.

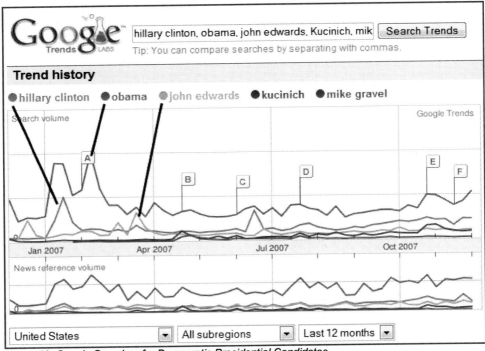

Image 16: Google Searches for Democratic Presidential Candidates

Notice how Barack Obama had a large amount of searches early in the year when he announced his candidacy for president. That is exactly what you would expect when someone with little national exposure is suddenly thrust into the national limelight.

The fact that the searches dropped off and didn't start rising again shows that people weren't interested in what they learned. Notice the same thing happened with Hillary Clinton. She gets spikes of interest that quickly drop off. This is a sign that an event occurred that temporarily drew interest. Real support would show a steady or increasing number of searches as people tell others.

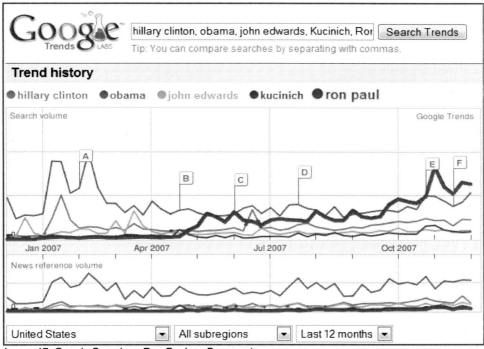

Image 17: Google Searches, Ron Paul vs. Democrats

Its clear that Ron Paul has more people searching for him than any of the other candidates, regardless of party. The official polls claim Hillary and Giuliani are the front runners but the larger more neutral results of Google searches shows Mike Huckabee and Mitt Romney ahead of Giuliani and Barack Obama ahead of Hillary Clinton.

Google searches don't mean people support that candidate. It means they are interested and are looking for information. To verify that interest reflects support its helpful to look at other measures as well.

Alexa.com provides three different perspectives of web popularity.

Combining this with Google I can determine what is real support and what is just curiosity.

Alexa has three measurements, Rank, Reach and Page Views. Rank measures number of visits to a web site. Sites are ranked in order against all others on the Internet. So a rank of 1 is the most popular web site on the Internet. Rank is similar to Google Searches but shows the people visited the specific website. Searches could be looking for any information about a candidate, good or bad. Visiting their web site is a stronger indication of support.

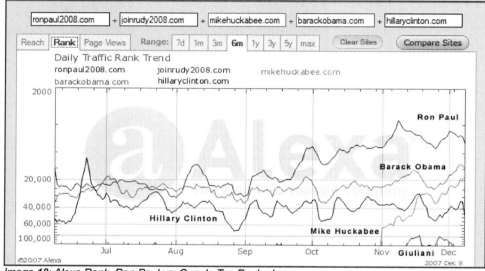

Image 18: Alexa Rank, Ron Paul vs. Google Top Ranked

The scale is logarithmic so Ron Paul's site is ranked 5 times as high as Barack Obama's or Mike Huckabee's website, 8 times higher than Hillary Clinton and 20 times higher than Giuliani.

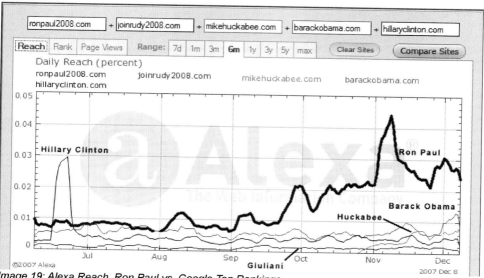

Image 19: Alexa Reach, Ron Paul vs. Google Top Rankings

Reach measures the number and variety of sites linking to the site measured. This is a very strong indicator of support since few people will post links to a candidate's site if they do not like that candidate.

Reach is also a good indicator of future growth. The more sites linking to your site the easier it is for people and search engine spiders to find your web site. Along with off-line introductions to Ron Paul's site, the huge amount of links fuels the exponential growth of supporters.

Notice the huge spike for Hillary Clinton in June, 2007. There was a lot of traffic to her site from many places then it dropped off. That is a horrible sign for her candidacy. Think of it this way, if you owned a restaurant and no one came back after your grand opening you won't stay in business for long. The extremely weak reach numbers show Hillary Clinton has practically no support. She will require large amounts of money for advertising and favorable media coverage to maintain her campaign.

Ron Paul needs very little money since he has huge natural sources of interest. And the exponential growth shows his message resonates with the people discovering him. The more people that discover Ron Paul, the more people support him and spread his message.

Page Views is the strongest indicator of support. People rarely read many pages on a web site they don't like. Page views can be higher if many

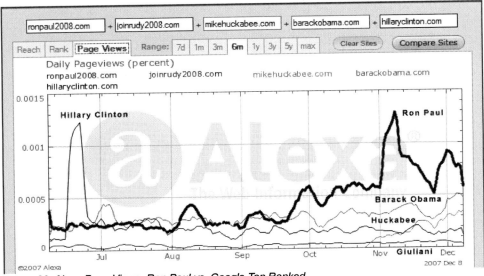

Image 20: Alexa Page Views, Ron Paul vs. Google Top Ranked

people read a single page or if few people read many pages. So you must look at Rank as well as Page Views to accurately assess interest and support.

Ron Paul's web site had a huge surge in page views on November 5th then it dropped off and rose sharply a few days later. On November 5th, 40,000 supporters went to his web site to make a donation. The next day there were 344 news articles and traffic to the site surged to double previous rates. After the excitement caused by the November 5th Money Bomb died down traffic, then sharply rose again within a week. This is exactly what you see when new people discover a web site and like it. They post links and tell their friends about it. The Money Bomb did more than collected $4.3 million it collected a huge number of new supporters.

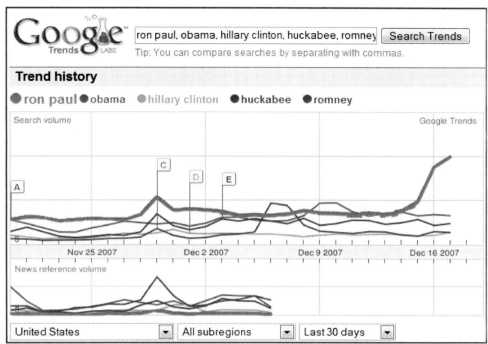

Image 21: Google Trends for Presidential Candidate the Day After the Tea Party

Note: The number of contributors for The Tea Party Money Bomb on December 16th was 50% more than November 5th. 40,000 people donated $4.3 million on November 5th. 60,000 people donated over $6 million. This external verification shows the exact same increase in support. Even more impressive is more than half of the contributors on December 16th had never contributed before. That is over 30,000 new contributors or 75% increase in support.

Ron Paul 2008
SECURE OUR BORDERS

Congressman Paul's Immigration Plan

1. Physically secure our borders and coastlines. We must do whatever it takes to control entry into our country.

2. Enforce visa rules. Immigration officials must track visa holders and deport anyone who overstays their visa or otherwise violates U.S. law.

3. No amnesty. Estimates suggest 10 to 20 million people are in our country illegally. That's a lot of people to reward for breaking our laws.

4. No welfare for illegal aliens. Taxpayers should not pay for illegal immigrants who use hospitals, clinics, schools, roads, and social services.

5. End birthright citizenship. As long as illegal immigrants know their children born here will be citizens, the incentive to enter the U.S. illegally will remain strong.

6. Pass true immigration reform. The current system is incoherent and unfair. But current reform proposals would allow up to 60 million more immigrants into our country.

"The talk must stop. We must secure our borders now. A nation without secure borders is no nation at all. It makes no sense to fight terrorists abroad when our own front door is left unlocked."   - Ron Paul

Image 22: Immigration Slim Jim

Ron Paul
FOR PRESIDENT 2008

Restore America's Sovereignty

The NAFTA superhighway is just one part of a plan to erase the borders between the U.S. and Mexico in order to form a North American Union.

This spawn of powerful special interests would create a single nation out of Canada, the U.S., and Mexico, with a new unelected bureaucracy and money system.

Forget about controlling immigration under this scheme -- and a free America, with limited, constitutional government, would be gone forever.

We must withdraw from any organizations and trade deals that infringe upon the freedom and independence of the United States of America.

Congressman Ron Paul is serving his 10th term in the U.S. House. He is a medical doctor who served his country as a Flight Surgeon in the Air Force and the Air National Guard. He never votes for any legislation unless it is expressly authorized by the Constitution.

www.RonPaul2008.com

Authorized and paid for by Ron Paul 2008 PCC

The Largest Minority

The industrial revolution focused on mass marketing. Success was achieved by making common items in the most cost efficient manner to sell to large groups of people. Standardization was the hallmark of the 19th and 20th century, but as the Information age emerged it became possible for the universal truth of individuality to move to the forefront. The potential for mass customization became reality and is totally revolutionizing every aspect of life. Oddly enough the information age, re-popularizes the ideas codified 230 years ago in the Constitution of the united States of America. The individual is King.

The Ron Paul Revolution benefits from a phenomenon described by what publisher of Wired magazine, Chris Anderson, calls "The Long Tail". In his article in Wired Magazine and his book of the same name, he pointed out that 98% of the Top 10,000 books carried by Amazon.com sell at least one copy per month. That means there is a market for every imaginable subject.

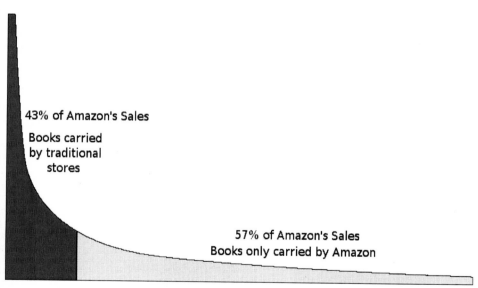

Image 23: Long Tail of Amazon's Book Sales

More importantly, Anderson exposed that only 43% of the sales were among the books carried by the traditional books stores. 57% of Amazon's sales came from the "long tail" of books that were not offered by traditional books stores. In other words, the unpopular fringe is actually the majority. The traditional book stores did not carry that 57% of books because, for them, sales were too low to be profitable. Amazon utilized the Internet to be more efficient so they could profitably sell a wider range of books.

Ron Paul's success is driven by the low cost of communication over the Internet and grassroots supporters evangelically spreading the message for free.

Normal party politics tries to aggregate people into groups to win voting blocks. Seeing people as part of a group is depersonalizing, it strips them of their true identity.

Amazon.com gives readers the freedom to choose from a selection of titles that traditional book stores never considered desirable. In political terms they were disenfranchised voters.

Ron Paul's message of freedom speaks to the smallest minority of all, the individual. Ron Paul speaks to you. And by definition, there are always more individuals than groups.

Several of the most hotly contended issues of our day revolve around one group wanting different treatment than another group. Gays want to openly serve in the military and get married. Atheists want government to forcibly remove religion from all public life. Some Christians want their religion actively supported by government. Other Christians want their religion protected from atheists trying to restrict them from practicing and other religions want the government to promote their religion. Women, blacks, and Hispanics want preferential consideration for admission to colleges and hiring for jobs.

Making one group happy always involves harming another. It just spirals out of control and no one is satisfied. Ron Paul's solution, the Constitutional solution, is to treat everyone as an individual. This gives everyone the most freedom and the most security.

Allowing individuals to choose for themselves reaches more people than treating people as groups. Ron Paul's message taps into the long tail of voters. In the USA, more than 50% of registered voters actually vote in a presidential election. In primaries the average turn out is 20%.

If Ron Paul can get 25% of the non-voting long tail to show up and vote for him, he will have more votes in the primary than all the other candidates combined. Realistically, Ron Paul only needs 5% of those untapped voters to win in the primaries.

The old thinking politicians believe the non-voters just don't care and won't show up. More likely the non-voters don't care for what they were offered by the old politicians. This is why the media and old politicians keep claiming the obviously large number of Ron Paul supporters don't exist. The old thinkers measure the old voters and don't find many Ron Paul supporters there. They completely ignore the overwhelming majority of untapped voters then claim that Ron Paul's large and growing support isn't real.

Traditional book stores and other retailers ignored and even ridiculed the Internet while Amazon and similar retailers tapped into the enormous unserved market. The traditional book sellers didn't even see it coming when Amazon became the largest retailer of books. The traditional book sellers were fighting over the existing market and ignoring an even larger market.

The online retailers offered what no one else could and grew the market. Not only did the online retailers offer lower prices than the traditional stores, they offered a wider selection that was easier to search. The Ron Paul Revolution is doing the same thing. Evangelism Marketing is spreading the message to an untapped audience and the lower cost allows the message to spread everywhere else for far less expense than the other politicians can afford.

The Ron Paul Revolution is growing exponentially the same way the Internet did.

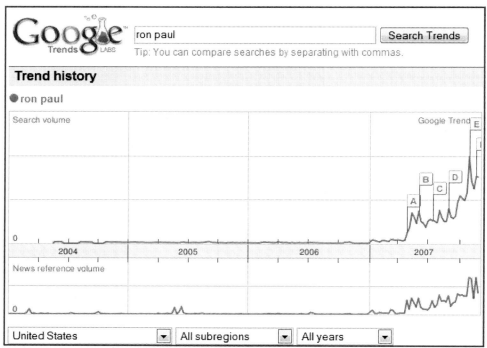

Image 24: Exponential Growth of Searches for Ron Paul

Undebatable Poll Results

According to polls, Ron Paul won every debate he's been in. During the first debate Rudolph Giuliani attacked Ron Paul about the war, claiming he'd never heard the reason that the terrorists attacked on 9/11 was because of 50 years of US military intervention in the Middle East. Ron Paul schooled Giuliani by quoting the official CIA report. The pundits claimed it was a big win for Giuliani but when the Text Messaging Polling results started coming in, Ron Paul resoundingly won the debate, getting 33% of the votes and more than twice as many as Giuliani.

During the commentary following the debate, Sean Hannity suggested people were voting multiple times even though Fox's voting system specifically prevented multiple votes from the same phone. The establishment couldn't understand how Ron Paul could be getting more votes than any other candidate.

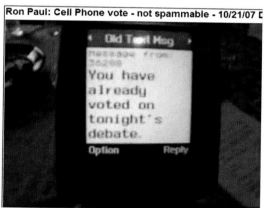

Image 25: SMS Poll, Not Spammable.
http://www.youtube.com/watch?v=y9LJZcdt9-k

How could a candidate saying things the media insiders didn't agree with have a lot of supporters? Corporate mainstream media is suppose to represent the majority. Fringe, unpopular ideas were suppose to be a minority. The long tail was wagging the dog.

Ron Paul won every time because he tapped into the hidden majority. People liked what he said and it was different. Ron Paul hit a nerve causing them to vote. Because it was remarkable, they called their friends and told them to watch and encouraged them to vote as well.

The hidden legions of Ron Paul supporters care more and are better informed than other candidate's supporters. Ron Paul's supporters knew when the debates were on and made sure to watch and vote. Now that everyone has cell phones, deep pocket supporters don't make as much difference. A million people that love your message so much they are willing to spend their own time and credibility promoting your message are worth more than a $100 million advertising budget.

Most cell phones have a feature to send a text message to a list of numbers. With the press of one button you can encourage 100 people to vote for Ron Paul. This technology leveled the field and helped create overwhelming group actions.

The live reporting of results of the text message polling also helped Ron Paul. Dedicated people were motivated to get more people to vote in order to push Ron Paul into the lead. And as others saw his numbers climbing they got involved in the excitement and also passed the message around. They formed an instant community around making Ron Paul win.

Free access to information helped promote freedom.

Image 26: Live Ron Paul Donation Meter Showing The Most Recent Donor

Its In The Air

A basic principle of Evangelism Marketing is seeding a message. If you reach the right people your message will spread to the rest of the population. Not all populations are connected, so the spread of the message can slow down and even stop. So you sometimes need to re-seed your message to reach other populations.

Once you reach enough people, another principle comes into play. Since we are all connected in some manner, once you reach enough people you achieve what's called the Tipping Point. Suddenly you reach everyone. It's like leaning back in your chair. You can lean back to a certain point and if you let go you return to a sitting position. But when you lean beyond the tipping point you tip completely over.

I had been monitoring the spread of Ron Paul's message and calculated how many people were being reached per day. Based on that rate we would not have enough to win the primary in Michigan on January 15th, 2008. I figured we needed to reach 50,000 people to achieve the tipping point. How could I do that with a limited budget?

Bouncing ideas around over the phone at midnight on Wednesday with the University of Michigan student coordinator, Adam deAngeli, we realized if we could share Ron Paul with everyone at a U of M football game we could reach 100,000 people in one day.

We tossed around a few ideas and came up with hiring an airplane to fly a banner around the game and have student supporters stand at the entrances with signs while handing out pamphlets.

First thing Thursday morning, I called companies to get prices for flying a banner around the stadium. I then created a ChipIn online fund raiser to get the money to make it happen. Within 8 hours we received enough contributions to pay for the plane. When the ChipIn was at the halfway point a single donor from California paid the rest of the money needed. A stranger on the other side of the country who only knew about the project from the posting on a web site contributed money to the cause.

When I called the airplane banner company on Friday, I discovered they were also Ron Paul supporters. This became a regular occurrence. Ron Paul supporters were everywhere. When people didn't know who Ron Paul was, if you talked to them a bit and then told them his positions on some issues important to them, you didn't need to say much more.

Saturday, the day of the event was electric. Myself and a camera operator arrived in town just as the planes were flying overhead. We met up with Adam & Alex near the gate to University of Michigan stadium and began filming.

Adam recently graduated from U of M with a degree in Computer Science. He ran a small shop catering to punk rockers, hip hop graffiti artists, and other counter culture fans. He grew up in a staunchly Democratic home and came to Ron Paul because of failings he saw with the socialist model of forcibly taking from one group to give to another. He'd made the website for the state wide Ron Paul campaign and dedicated all his free time to supporting Ron Paul.

Alex was attending business school and rented professional lights and audio equipment to bands and people hosting events. Alex's background was more traditionally conservative. He values Ron Paul for consistently

following the ideal the Republicans had claimed to support. Adam and Alex have very different personalities backgrounds and lifestyles but came together to support freedom and Ron Paul.

Adam and Alex handed out leaflets to the thousands of people going into the stadium. After handing out all the leaflets we started walking through the crowds while Alex carried a Ron Paul sign on a pole for everyone to see.

Literally hundreds of people shouted their support for Ron Paul. When I would ask people that shouted, "why do you like Ron Paul", they all had thoughtful well informed answers. We were amazed by how much genuine admiration existed for Ron Paul.

What we saw did not match the reports on the news. We couldn't walk 10 feet without someone shouting out support for Ron Paul. It was an incredible rush having so many people respond so positively.

We made two videos of the event and posted them both on YouTube. The first one received 15,000 views within the first week and became the most popular video in several categories and would lead to changes in the official campaign.

Dr. Paul, I Presume

In September 2007 before the Republican Leadership Conference the Ron Paul campaign had no idea how much support they really had. Most people didn't really know.

When I attended a special fund raising dinner I was given my first opportunity to meet Ron Paul. I brought a DVD with the video of the University of Michigan vs. Notre Dame football game Airplane Banner event to show them. I had the restaurant staff play it on the big screen TV. When it came on, everyone including Ron Paul were stunned. Ron Paul kept asking me where and when the video was filmed and he asked his staff if they knew about it.

That night I got to spend an hour talking to Ron Paul one on one. He is a very smart man and really really knows a lot about the nation. Anyone that's earned an M.D. Is smart. Ron Paul goes far beyond that having six books published on economics and national policy.

Image 27: Ron Paul and Mark Frazier

The most impressive thing I discovered by meeting Dr. Paul and talking with him in person is how real he is. I've met most of the other presidential candidates and I've met many celebrities including rock musicians like Ted Nugent. Most people that depend on popularity for their career try to gain attention. Whether its conscious or not they present themselves in a way to get attention.

Ron Paul is very different. When I walked into the room I had to ask someone where Ron Paul was. They pointed to a table in the corner where he was sitting. I walked over and said hello. He said hello and asked me to sit and just started talking to me. Absolutely no pretense or anything fake at all. He is very unassuming and easy to talk to. That might be one of the reasons he was such a good obstetrician. I imagine delivering over 4,000 babies requires a great bed side manner. He has it.

I learned from his staff that Ron Paul is naturally quite introverted. And from what I experienced I believe it. When he jokes about wanting to be president of Switzerland because no one knows who the president of

Switzerland is, he's saying as much about his personality as his political philosophy.

In addition to showing Ron Paul and members of his staff the video, I showed them Google Trends graphs indicating he had more support than all the other Republicans and was the only Republican that could beat Hillary Clinton. This was powerful information to receive two days before the Republican Leadership Conference in Mackinac.

Most Republicans talk about Hillary Clinton getting elected as being the worst thing possible. Since the real data clearly shows Ron Paul is the only Republican candidate that would win against Hillary, it has a very big impact.

Image 28: University of Michigan Supports Ron Paul
http://www.youtube.com/watch?v=BFy--JHgYlw

The Revolution Will Not Be Televised

"You will not be able to stay home, brother.
You will not be able to plug in, turn on and cop out.
You will not be able to lose yourself on skag and skip,
Skip out for beer during commercials,
Because the revolution will not be televised..."

When Gil Scott-Heron recorded his now famous poem on the 1970 album "Small Talk at 125 and Lenox" he didn't foresee YouTube. Radicals from the era of flower power realized the mass media licensed by government and controlled by big business wasn't representing reality.

Back in 1970 no one would've considered Ron Paul revolutionary or radical. Only a few years earlier he was serving in the military during the Vietnam War as a flight surgeon. Now today what made him conservative is being called radical.

In 1517 Martin Luther nailed his revolutionary 95 Theses to the church door questioning the corruption he saw with the Roman Catholic Church. When he did that, he started a movement fueled by Gutenberg's invention of the printing press. Printed copies of his 95 Theses spread all over Europe. And the printing press allowed common people to break free from their dependence on priests to interpret the Bible. Gutenberg made it possible for anyone to read the truth of the Bible themselves.

The Internet, through YouTube, Google, and many other video sites, now lets anyone search for the truth to see with their own eyes. No more dependence on the talking heads to filter and interpret events. The Internet expands the distributed creation and delivery of information similar to how the printing press did.

When books were expensive the flow of information was easy to control. Only the people that could afford scribes to manually make copies could make books to spread their message. The centralization of information creation and distribution created excessive power in the hands of the information elite. The printing press drastically reduced the cost of spreading the message to large audiences.

Television and radio followed the same progression of being very expensive and controlled by a few people. Both made it possible for more people to be reached more quickly but it centralized the flow of information. The Internet distributed the ability to share information. Now just about anyone can broadcast audio and video to just about anyone else everywhere in the world. The pyramid has been flattened.

Now that anyone can post the video of what really happened to YouTube the entire world can see it instantly. The Internet even distributes interpretation.

You've probably heard the saying, "A picture is worth a thousand words." If that is true you can only imagine how many words video is worth. Until recently video was extremely expensive. Today digital video cameras and editing software are cheap and easy to use. With the advent of YouTube and similar video sites the amateur can sometimes beat the TV crews to airing their video.

Citizen journalism has totally changed media. No longer are people stuck with the official version. No longer are stories stuck in the back pages or not even covered at all. A normal person with a video camera can capture what actually happened and have it online for the entire world to see within minutes. And when people see the important stories they quickly spread them causing an avalanche of attention.

YouTube has been a major part of the Ron Paul Revolution. People share videos they recorded or made to promote Ron Paul's message, post comments to those videos and link to other videos to help educate others about everything related to the freedom movement.

As of December 1, 2007 there are over 60,000 videos related to Ron Paul posted on YouTube. Ron Paul is so popular, a few unscrupulous people trying to get attention for totally unrelated items, put Ron Paul in the title knowing that will increase views.

YouTube is one of the major ways Ron Paul supporters communicate with each other. They encourage each other by showing how many people attend an event. They train supporters by showing techniques that have worked.

The video I made of the airplane flying a banner over the University of Michigan stadium football game received 14,000 views the first week and sparked a nation wide event. Ron Paul supporters at other colleges used the friendly rivalry to match what we did at the University of Michigan. This led to 11 colleges all flying banners on the same day. Students from opposing teams joined together to support Ron Paul.

Poor Mitt Romney chose to have an event at Michigan State University the same day Ron Paul had events at 11 universities nationwide including Michigan State. The Ron Paul supporters didn't want Mitt to feel lonely with only a couple dozen paid staff showing up to his free BBQ. I bet you didn't see that on TV. The Revolution isn't always televised but it is on YouTube.

Ron Paul Tailgate!

Image 29: Mitt Romney at Michigan State University
http://www.youtube.com/watch?v=tbg4nPMU088

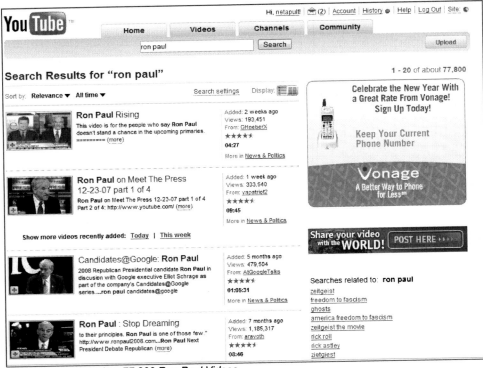

Image 30: YouTube has 77,800 Ron Paul Videos

Fox News "Crap Like That"

People that typically vote for Republican candidates complain about liberal bias in media. Fox News claims to counter act the liberal media bias with "fair and balanced" reporting. CNN being caught reporting faked events lends credence to the concept of liberal bias. Of course people that like the CNN stories, even if fake, ridicule Fox News as being a propaganda engine for the Republican Party.

When Ron Paul totally shook up the first Fox News Republican Party debate by questioning the validity of the reasoning for invading Iraq he was openly attacked by the hosts. Only after the Text Messaging Polling results came in did they start changing their tune. People sensitive to media bias noticed but others discounted their objections as only being subjective personal opinion.

It was odd because Ron Paul was actually making the most conservative, most republican statement of all the candidates. And his statements were backed up by official government documents and the US Constitution itself.

Whether the media is on your side or not doesn't matter for an Evangelism Marketing campaign. All that matters is you publish your message and get it in the hands of people that will spread it.

Camera crews at the Mackinac Republican Leadership Conference caught a local Fox News Anchorman on camera telling his crew "Get people eating and crap like that but don't show all the Ron Paul supporters." When a copy of that video was published to the Internet it spread like wild fire.

The video made it to the first page of Digg.com the hugely popular Web 2.0 site. The interactive community allows users to vote to Digg or Bury news items and ranks the stories based on the shared opinion of the community. The first page of Digg.com gets millions of views per day so stories on the first page get a lot of attention.

The story also was posted on the first page of controversial alternative media heavy weight Alex Jones's website Prison Planet. Say what you want about Alex Jones, he is popular. Being featured on his web site or radio show generates a lot of traffic.

The video received 100,000 views within minutes.

Many people had complained about the treatment Ron Paul was getting from Fox News but seeing active censorship with your own eyes was shocking.

From that point on the corporate media stopped ignoring Ron Paul and actively attacked him. They couldn't ignore the fact that Ron Paul supporters were everywhere with video cameras and would expose the truth.

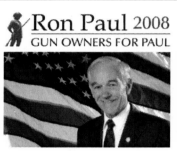

"I share our Founders' belief that in a free society each citizen must have the right to keep and bear arms. They ratified the Second Amendment knowing that this right is the guardian of every other right."
                                    - Congressman Ron Paul

Ron Paul's Pro-Gun Record:

- Authored H.R. 1096, which repeals the Brady Handgun Violence Prevention Act and the Federal Firearms License Reform Act of 1993.

- Authored H.R. 1697, which would end the ban on carrying a firearm in the National Park System, restoring Americans' ability to protect themselves in potentially hazardous situations.

- Authored H.R. 3305, which would allow pilots and specially assigned law enforcement personnel to carry firearms in order to protect airline passengers, possibly preventing future 9/11-style attacks.

- Authored H.R. 1146, which would end our membership in the United Nations, protecting us from its attempts to tax our guns or disarm us entirely.

- Introduced legislation to repeal the so-called assault weapons ban before its 2004 sunset. He opposes any attempts to reinstate it.

He also recently opposed H.R. 2640, which would create and expand massive federal government databases and violate the medical privacy of all our citizens.

You have the right to protect your life, liberty, and property. As President, Dr. Paul will continue to guard your Second Amendment liberties.

http://GunOwners.RonPaul2008.com
Authorized and paid for by Ron Paul 2008 PCC

Ron Paul: Restore the Constitution

- No National ID Card/Backdoor Gun Registration
- No Assault Weapon Ban
- No Mandated Trigger Locks
- No Tax Dollars to the Anti-Gun United Nations

"Considering all of the 2008 Presidential candidates, Democrat or Republican, Dr. Ron Paul is the only one I trust to protect our right to keep and bear arms without compromise." - Dr. Stephen C. King, past president of Gun Owners of New Hampshire

"Dr. Paul gets it. He supports our gun rights because it's right - not just expedient. You can count on him always to do that. With every other candidate our gun rights are secondary." - Ed Kelleher, President, GrassRoots South Carolina, Inc.

"Ron Paul has been a leader in the fight to defend and restore the 2nd Amendment." - Larry Pratt, Exec. Director, Gun Owners of America

Congressman Ron Paul is serving his 10th term in the U.S. House. Dr. Ron Paul has assisted women in delivering over 4,000 babies. He served his country as a Flight Surgeon in the Air Force and the Air National Guard. Congressman Paul never votes for any legislation unless it is expressly authorized by the Constitution.

To Defend One Part of the Constitution, We Must Defend All of It!

Image 31: Gun Owners Slim Jim

Remember, Remember the 5th of November

"Remember, Remember the 5th of November" was the rallying call for Ron Paul supporters who joined together and set the record for the amount of money raised on a single day for any candidate during a primary.

Unless you're from the United Kingdom, the phrase Remember, Remember the 5th of November is a line from the movie "V for Vendetta". The movie is the fictional tale of "V", the victim of a totally corrupt military dictatorship who motivates thousands of citizens to stand up for freedom by hijacking the TV network to expose the lies the government was telling.

The event was referred to as a money bomb, a way to prove Ron Paul's support was real. Instead of using violence as in the movie, Ron Paul supporters would break through the wall of silence and spin that was claiming Ron Paul's massive support was only an Internet prank.

> November 5th Money Bomb raised $4.3 million in 24 hours

On November 5, 2007 several records were set. In a 24 hour period over 38,000 normal people donated on average $100 each, raising $4.3 million. That was 30% more money than the previous record and 60 times as many people donating. It thoroughly proved Ron Paul has a lot of real supporters.

Until this point the main stream media mostly ignored Ron Paul or discounted him as not being a real candidate and only having a few online supporters that were faking the appearance of a lot of support. When the money came rolling in it changed a lot of things. November 6th Ron Paul received 344 news articles. This created a huge surge in traffic to his web site.

One month after the money bomb he collected another $4 million. I suspect the extra attention from the November 5th money bomb generated a lot of extra donations.

Even though we broke through the wall of silence the media still negatively spun the event. The mainstream media linked it to the British celebration of Guy Fawkes Day claiming its when a foiled terrorist attack from the 1600's occurred. Even though "V for Vendetta" referenced Guy

Fawkes day the November 5th Ron Paul Money Bomb was more about how the character in the movie got people to see the truth than a celebration in the UK.

Additionally, the media simply didn't understand what was going on. They first asked the Ron Paul campaign how they organized it but true to form Ron Paul told the truth and said he had nothing to do with it. Still looking for some top down organized structure they claimed it was the work of Trevor Lyman who set up a website promoting the event.

The truth is it was the result of a lot of individuals sharing ideas to help the cause. During October a lot of people were trying to come up with ways to prove Ron Paul's support was real. The idea of everyone donating money on the same day was floating around in chat rooms and on forums for a while. Since November 5th was approaching someone suggested that day because of the movie and it just took off. Trevor setup a web site to help with the efforts that were already underway to promote it. The only reason it got the attention it did was because of many many people spreading the word. It really was grassroots.

Even after the fact when Trevor Lyman told PBS – NOW that it wasn't his idea and he was only one person among many that made it happen, PBS still didn't get it. All the media and the old politicians saw it as being controlled from the top down. They just don't understand individuals freely doing things. And they certainly don't understand individuals freely working together without any central planning or organization. Freedom works.

The people in the media aren't the only ones that don't understand what they are seeing. The campaign professionals on Ron Paul's staff completely miss the boat on every detail.

November 5th proved that Ron Paul supporters weren't just a small group of people online. There were a large number of real people willing to spend their money. They had already been spending their time. More importantly it showed these people would show up to make a difference.

The Ron Paul staffers don't even understand the real significance of the November 5th Money Bomb. In a conversation I had with National Field Director Denis Fusaro, he said, "The Internet is mostly independents and they won't show up to vote in a Republican primary. We are focusing on delegates and registered Republicans who voted in the last primary." He said, "40,000 people isn't enough people, we need millions." As politely as I could I tried to tell him the Money Bomb was just the tip of an ice burg. Donating $100 is a lot larger commitment than voting. I tried to convince him that Ron Paul has massive support and all we needed to do was increase name recognition. I also offered him a way to reach every household in the United States before the primaries and do it for $0.01 per household. He flat out refused saying, "Unless you can give me cheap direct mailing rates then I'm not interested. I've been doing Republican campaigns for years and direct mail is what works."

This isn't a Republican campaign, its a freedom campaign. And any so called experience from years ago was worse than useless it was deadly. Ron Paul would do much better to hire professional marketers than the political activists he has hired. Fortunately the grassroots has many very good professional marketers with real experience in the new distributed communication driven world. But this also is bad. Despite all the bumbling and destructive actions of the professional political staff, things are succeeding better than he had hoped. So I suspect the political staff is taking credit for results they didn't create but actually hindered.

Tea Party, December 16, 2007

Hoping to duplicate the enthusiasm of the November 5 Money Bomb another one was immediately planned for the anniversary of the Boston Tea Party when colonists threw the shipment of tea in to the Boston harbor in protest of the tax imposed on them by King George of England.

The hope of the Tea Party is to break the record again but I believe something more significant is occurring. People across Europe are holding their own event in support of their American brothers and sisters. They will be rallying in Strasbourg France outside the European Parliament building.

Ron Paul isn't just a presidential candidate, he is the spokesman for a message with universal appeal. The freedom message brings people together.

The videos and blogs made by people outside the USA are some of the most moving. They live in nations with far less freedom and with far worse economic conditions than the USA and they are begging us to avoid their fate and express how much they want Ron Paul's message to spread in their nations the way it is spreading in the USA.

By the time this is published the Tea Party will have occurred. I hope it goes very well but I have concerns. I'm not concerned that it won't raise a lot of money. It will raise millions.

My concern is that the Tea Party won't receive the same kind of press as the November 5th Money Bomb. If the same amount of money is raised it really isn't news. The media will look at it as more of the same. Even if a new record is set, if it isn't a lot more, then it still isn't front page news.

I've spoken to many dedicated supporters from around the nation and they are fed up with the political staffers mismanaging the campaign. They are investing their money into grassroots projects like the Ron Paul Blimp, Billboards for Iowa and other projects completely outside the control of the staffers.

If enough people choose to not donate, the media might spin the Tea Party as Ron Paul losing support. The exact opposite is the reality. They are following the message of freedom and making the correct decisions.

One extremely dedicated supporter told me, "I was planning to send another $1100 but now I wish I had not sent the money I did. Its much better spent on projects at the grassroots level." If 1,000 other big contributors feel the same then the Tea Party will be short $1 million.

We will see what happens. One thing for sure. These people are not turning back on freedom. They've proven to themselves and everyone else in the freedom movement that they can do it. Even if Ron Paul is not elected, the Revolution will live on worldwide.

Truth Sells Itself

Before the November 5th money bomb I had asked my brother to provide a quote for some special marketing assistance. Because the Michigan Primary was in legal limbo I wanted to send a mailing to all the delegates.

My brother runs a marketing firm that specializes in fund raising for non-profit organizations. He told me how much it would cost and also that Fred Thompson had contacted him but had not yet signed a contract.

After closely considering what my brother could offer I chose not to pay for the service. I'm very glad because it turns out we didn't need it.

The primary will go on as planned. More importantly we raised more money in less time with less expense than the cheapest rate my brother could offer.

Because Ron Paul's message is true, its evangelical. Fred Thompson has to spend 85% more to spread his message than Ron Paul.

And Fred Thompson has been trying to copy Ron Paul's message. But no one can match Ron Paul's 20 year voting record. Also because Ron Paul is simply telling the truth and not delivering a planned speech he doesn't get tripped up by questions.

If you always tell the truth you never have to memorize your lines. That works in Ron Paul's favor because he isn't the most polished speaker. His only desire is to see the nation return to the freedom we once had. Restore the Constitution, peace, and prosperity.

The common opinion is a presidential campaign requires gigantic fortunes. That just isn't true. Mass media can help speed the seeding of a message but it spreads from person to person. If one day you told 5 people the same message and everyone that heard it repeated it to 5 people the message would reach 244 million people in 12 days. Nearly the entire population of the USA could be reached in less than 2 weeks simply by each person telling 5 new people. Now add on to that cell phones and the Internet and you see a message could reach the entire USA in minutes without spending one cent on mass media.

Days   # People

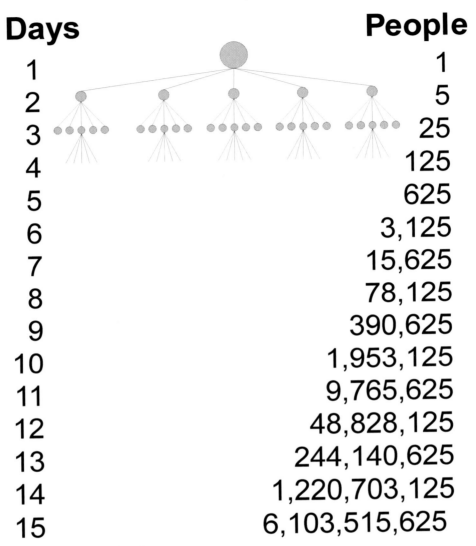

Days	People
1	1
2	5
3	25
4	125
5	625
6	3,125
7	15,625
8	78,125
9	390,625
10	1,953,125
11	9,765,625
12	48,828,125
13	244,140,625
14	1,220,703,125
15	6,103,515,625

Image 32: Geometric Growth

Worth His Weight in Gold & Silver

One of the biggest problems facing the world today is inflation. Fuel, health care, housing, practically everything is costing more and more. Ron Paul is the only presidential candidate talking about the cause of the problem and he is the only one dedicated to solving it.

This is an issue that can be very confusing. It is intentionally confusing because the fact is you are being robbed and the thieves don't want you to know.

Ron Paul has had a running battle with the Federal Reserve Chairman. Now that the financial system of the entire world is collapsing Ron Paul isn't pulling any punches. Many people first learned about the real situation with our monetary system by reading what Ron Paul wrote or hearing him grilling Alan Greenspan or Ben Bernake when they testified before congress.

Ron Paul wants to make sure your money keeps its value. This is what he means when he says "sound money". And Ron Paul wants to end the "inflation tax" that steals the value of your money right out of your pocket without you even seeing it happening to you.

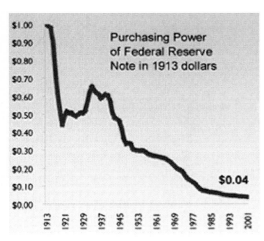

If your money doesn't buy anything you are in trouble. The last time this happened it led to World War II. In Germany people literally had to carry their money around in wheel barrels because it cost so much to buy anything. This is exactly what is happening today. The money isn't worth as much as it was before.

There are two types of inflation, real and monetary. Real inflation is always temporary and is solved by technology increasing productivity or people simply changing their preferences. Monetary inflation is created through deceptive banking practices.

Very few people understand the real causes of inflation so its hard to take the facts seriously. Most people just don't want to believe something so obviously fraudulent could go on. Just remember, it didn't happen all at once and once it starts happening you either suffer a little to fix it or suffer a huge amount later when it all comes crashing down.

Real inflation occurs when there is less of a product than what people want. Real inflation typically happens when more people want an item than what can be produced. People moving into a town drives up prices for property in that town and lowers it in the places they move from. Real inflation also can happen temporarily from an increase in population or because of something that caused productivity to decrease such as an earthquake. But more people means more labor and in time they make more of the things to satisfy the needs.

Monetary inflation happens when the money isn't worth as much as it was. Monetary inflation is caused by the supply of money increasing. How does that happen?

Imagine if when ever you wanted something you would just print money to buy it. You could act like you are the richest person in the world. And as long as people kept giving you what you wanted in exchange for the money you created from nothing things would be great for you. But over time as the amount of money you printed increased everyone would have it and they would stop selling you things for the money you created. You would have debased the currency.

Throughout time governments have debased the currency in order to buy things when they could not raise the money through taxes. The word debase means to base the money on something less valuable. Gold and silver have been used for thousands of years. When governments debased the currency they would mix the gold or silver with cheaper metals and eventually replace the gold or silver altogether with cheap junk like tin. Its like giving you glass and telling you its a diamond.

Today in the United States coins are plated zinc. And even though zinc is one of the cheapest metals in the world the amount used in a penny is worth more than $0.01. The US government recently passed a law banning melting pennies and nickels down for their metal value. Can you imagine having something so worthless that the cheap junk metal its made of is worth more? But it wasn't long ago that US coins were gold and silver.

Using cheap metals for coins is bad, but its nothing compared to paper money. There is practically no limit to how low the value can go when you just print pieces of paper and claim they are money. Now that most money isn't even printed but just numbers stored in computers there isn't any limit at all.

Governments aren't the only ones that create money and debase the currency. Banks can do it as well and the way they do it is very sneaky.

Banks create money by loaning it out with interest. They use all sorts of manipulation to hide what is going on but when they loan you money with interest they steal from someone else.

Think of it this way. If there is $100 in the world and I loan you that $100 for 10% interest, you must pay me back $110 when the loan is due. Where does that extra $10 come from? No where, you can't pay back the interest because you never

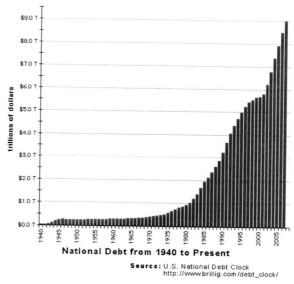

National Debt from 1940 to Present

Source: U.S. National Debt Clock
http://www.brillig.com/debt_clock/

received it to begin with. Unless I am willing to accept payment in something other than dollars then its impossible for you to pay the interest. Of course it would be stupid to not take something else. Bankers know this and have a method to deal with it.

The way bankers deal with you defaulting on the loan is to require collateral, like your house or car. If you don't pay back the loan plus the interest the bank takes your property you pledged as collateral. You lose your house or car and the banker gets it. They traded you money they created from nothing for your house.

Why haven't you heard this before? The fact the interest is impossible to pay back is hidden because there are lots of people exchanging money for real items like food, land, and labor. The system works for a while as long as you can get money from someone else to pay the interest to the banker.

But eventually someone gets stuck with paying all the interest created from nothing.

Some people might say, the banker charges interest to compensate for risk. But that misses the point. Since the interest does not exist its impossible to pay it back so someone will eventually lose their property.

Shouldn't we be seeing this all the time? We do but its not right out in the open. It doesn't happen right away because they don't loan out all the money at once and because the terms of the loans are for many years. It takes time before the credit bubble bursts. The USA and the entire world are now experiencing the credit bubble bursting.

When the bubble bursts people stuck with loans lose their property. The first people this happens to are poor people. So when you hear talk about Sub-Prime Mortgages its really just the first step in a big collapse.

When the banks take the property away what happens to the money? The banks write it off. The interest disappears and the total supply of money shrinks. This makes it harder for other people to get money to pay off their loans and the entire system cascades into a collapse.

If this sounds horrible you are correct. The Great Depression was caused by bankers collapsing the money supply. Even though there was plenty of real stuff in the world there wasn't enough money for people to use to buy it. People were out in the streets without jobs while factories were sitting empty. If you drive through the industrial cities in the US today you see the same thing.

Shouldn't the whole system collapse quickly enough to see it? Yes. There is an even worse part of the system that hides what is really going on and makes the eventual collapse even worse. Its called fractional reserve banking.

When a banker loans you money and requires interest he created that interest out of nothing. Until you are required to pay back the loan plus interest nobody sees what happened. The economy has $100. The extra $10 only exists on paper with the banker.

A long time ago goldsmiths saw a similar thing happening with people that deposited their gold for safe keeping. The goldsmiths would give them receipts for their gold but the people wouldn't collect the gold very often. It was easier for them to trade the receipts. The goldsmiths realized they could print more receipts than they had real gold and no one would know. This works just fine because only a fraction of the gold is ever collected. That was the beginning of banking as we know it today.

Fractional reserve bankers create more receipts than they have gold and then loan out those worthless receipts for interest. Now the banker isn't only collecting interest that doesn't exist he is loaning you principle that doesn't exist.

Fractional reserve banking solved a big problem for the bankers. It is impossible to pay back the interest. The people taking out loans needed a way to get more money. With fractional reserve banking the bankers could print the money themselves. The borrower is happy because they get to buy things they can't afford and the banker is happy because they create money to buy things. What happened is the banker and the borrower stole the value of the money from everyone else.

If a hard working person saves up $100 worth of gold and deposits it in the bank, the banker gives the depositor a receipt for the gold. The banker has lots of depositors and he knows that only 10% of them collect their gold at one time. So the banker knows he can safely loan out 90% of the money and still have enough on hand to give to the few depositors that collect their gold.

When a banker loans out $90 he gives a receipt for $90 to the borrower and writes down he has $100 on deposit and is owed another $90. He now claims to have $190 worth of money but he still only has the original $100 worth of gold. What happened is the banker and the borrower cut in half the value of the hard working person's receipts.

The borrower is happy because he goes and buys stuff with this worthless paper which quickly causes the prices of everything to rise. The hard working depositor sees prices rising and doesn't know what happened. The hard working depositor might even think this was good. He can sell his property for more money. On paper he thinks he is getting richer. When he tries to buy something he realizes something is wrong but can't tell if it is real inflation or monetary inflation.

Of course we don't even use cash most of the time. People write checks. This further hides the fact the real money, the gold isn't there. Bankers can even keep the receipts and never have any gold at all.

Only if the depositors take their gold out of the bank is the real problem uncovered and the banker is bankrupt. Many people taking their money out at the same time is called a run on the bank and that is exactly what happened during the Great Depression. When many people started taking their money out, the banks couldn't pay and the entire system collapsed.

Since 1913, when the Federal Reserve started creating money it has lost 97% of its value. Your great great grandfather would only have to work one day to earn enough money to buy what now takes you a month to earn. That is why people used to be able to save enough money to buy homes for cash but now it takes 30 years to pay for a home.

Prior to 1913 the United States Treasury printed certificates that were redeemable in gold or silver and minted coins that were made of valuable metals. At any time you could redeem the paper for gold or silver. Because the Treasury had to have gold or silver to pay you when you demanded it, the value of the paper money stayed the same.

In 1913 a private corporation owned by a group of banks was given a monopoly to issue money. The Federal Reserve is a private bank, they decide how much money will be in circulation and then get it printed. The Federal Reserve does not do the actual printing. They hire the Department of Engraving to make the actual piece of paper but the Federal Reserve then sells those Federal Reserve Notes to the US Treasury for Treasury Bills. This is where the national debt comes from.

Look at the money in your pocket. It says "Federal Reserve Note". Dollars used to say, "Silver Certificate" and payable on demand. Today they are

Image 33: One Dollar Silver Certificate

worthless pieces of paper backed by nothing.

Treasury Bills are loans with interest. But rather than loaning all the money the Treasury Bills are sold at a discount. This means the face value might be $100 but you purchase it for $70. When the treasury bill matures the United States Treasury now must pay you $100. The problem with this is the treasury only had $70. In order to get the extra $30 to pay you it must borrow more money. So the endless cycle of debt runs out of control.

Does this sound complicated? Its suppose to be. The American people were not supposed to figure out what was going on. Central banks have always done this type of thing and if people knew what was happening they would have stopped it instantly.

President Andrew Jackson was famous for stopping a central bank from gaining control of the United States money. When asked what his greatest accomplishment was he said, "I killed the bank". Its disgusting that his face is now on a worthless piece of paper issued by the largest central bank ever.

Does tricking people into giving up their property sound like fraud? It is. So why isn't the government stopping it? The government isn't stopping it because they are the worst abuser of the system. If government tries to tax people too much the people simply refuse to pay or even revolt. Its much easier for the government to borrow money and push the cost along to people through the banking system.

When governments debase the currency its obvious quite quickly. People immediately turn to other forms of money, typically gold or silver. People use gold and silver as money because the government can't take away its value. That quickly puts an end to the government debasing the currency.

If there is competing currency then people can use that to avoid the fraud of the debased money. For thousand's of years gold and silver have always been what people turn to when the currency is debased.

Paying taxes is the only reason people need the government currency. Banks can't debase the currencies without the help of government.

Central banks create money from nothing and then loan this fictional money to governments causing an endless cycle of debt. Since the government owes interest and was only loaned the principle its impossible to ever pay off the debt. Governments keep borrowing more and more to just pay the ever increasing interest.

As more and more money is created it becomes worth less and less. So it seems like prices are rising when in reality its money losing value. Worthless paper, or now digits in a computer, don't float, they sink like a rock.

This "inflation tax" is the most destructive tax of all because it literally steals money right out of the pockets of poor and middle class by reducing the purchasing power of the money you own.

Historically the only way to avoid this type of devaluing of the currency is to have it backed by gold and silver. In fact the word "dollar" is a unit of weight in gold. If you go back in time 1 ounce of gold had the same purchasing power as it does today. 2000 years ago in Rome, an ounce of gold would buy you a nice suit, a belt, and shoes. Today, an ounce of gold will buy you a nice suit, belt and shoes. Gold has kept its value.

In 1998 Bernard von NotHaus formed Liberty Dollar to create gold and silver coins that really were dollars. In addition to minting coins they issued warehouse receipts backed with gold and silver. Legally it wasn't competition for the worthless Federal Reserve notes we call money because no one was required to take it. Of course anyone refusing pure gold or silver in trade would be an idiot. Everyday people trade useful items from baseball cards, to cars and even houses. Trading these collectible items isn't only perfectly legal, its a wise investment.

Ron Paul is well known for supporting sound money. In celebration of The 4th of July, 2007 Liberty Dollar honored Ron Paul by minting coins featuring his face. These pure gold and silver coins and warehouse receipts circulated for nearly

RON PAUL DOLLAR

10 years constantly increasing in value as prices for gold and silver rose. Liberty Dollar minted the coin without any involvement or permission from Ron Paul.

After close to a decade of operation, suddenly in 2007 when Ron Paul's campaign was achieving success, the FBI raided Liberty Dollar confiscating 4 tons of gold worth millions of dollars and all the records leaving no way to refund customers for unfulfilled orders.

Ron Paul supporters were outraged at the clear violation of law. The corporate media reported on the raid with headlines like "Ron Paul Funny Money Confiscated" implying the pure gold and silver were somehow counterfeit. Since at the time the Liberty Dollar was raided gold was selling at over $830 per ounce and silver was over $15 per ounce, implying the coins with Ron Paul's face on them were illegitimate was ludicrous. The reality was Liberty Dollars were real money and the Federal Reserve Notes were worthless pieces of paper redeemable for nothing.

As soon as the story came out hundreds of posts were made to all the news sites and people were calling into radio programs and TV shows stating the facts. The story quickly dropped from site just like the gold and silver taken from Liberty Dollar.

It was a wake up call to Ron Paul supporters in the USA. The powers that be would play hard ball. It proved that Ron Paul was viewed as a threat to the establishment. This increased the resolve of supporters to get Ron Paul elected and put an end to this type of tyranny.

Illustration 1: Liberty Dollar Warehouse Receipts & Coin

Ron Paul Brings People Together

The rivalry between University of Michigan and Ohio State University is legendary. In 1835 Michigan and Ohio went to war over control of Toledo. The war was avoided but U of M and Ohio State University have been battling on the football field ever since.

U of M vs. OSU is such a big event that ESPN Game Day broadcast live from the game. Extra police are on duty to handle the numerous fights between football fans on the opposing sides. So when the two schools joined together to support Ron Paul it was impressive. Students from both schools raised donations to pay for airplanes to fly over the stadium saying their school supported Ron Paul for President. A group of students from both schools

U of M and OSU Support Ron Paul
http://www.youtube.com/watch?v=Nk2BoPuAqGw

began waiting at 6 am for a spot to be on TV. Their dedication was rewarded with several clear displays on national TV of their banner saying, "OSU & UM Support Ron Paul for President."

There was a large number of Ron Paul supporters from both schools holding huge banners. When you turn the corner to the road leading the stadium you could see 4x8ft sign the entire way to the gate.

Once every one had entered the stadium we walked across town to our vehicles. We had to carry these 4x8ft signs 10 blocks. As we walked we were stunned by people rushing out of their homes to tell us they supported Ron Paul. This happened on every single block. It was great.

There are militant atheists and very devout Christians who join together to support Ron Paul. Seventy year olds and teenagers, high school drop outs and college professors all getting together to discuss and work to get Ron Paul elected.

You don't see that with other candidate's. Even if wide ranges of people support the other candidate's they don't put aside their differences to give support. That is unique for the freedom message of Ron Paul.

Why Blacks & People of Color Should Vote for Ron Paul

http://www.youtube.com/watch?v=7ji_Ft23BDw

One of the attempted ridiculous slurs against Ron Paul claims that he is racist. They usually refer to a 20 year old article written by a staff member of a newsletter that Ron Paul allowed to use his name. The article is misinterpreted plus they usually fail to mention the staff member was fired.

RON PAUL: Why Blacks & People Of Color Should Vote

Cry for Ron Paul - BelgiansForPaul

http://www.youtube.com/watch?v=Az2lhPhBCUo

Ron Paul's support is international. A group of Belgians create a very well produced video detailing how much worse off their country is and that they want Ron Paul's ideas to take hold in their nation.

Deutschland - Wer ist Ron Paul?

http://www.youtube.com/watch?v=OFoAKDh1F0s

Germans seeking freedom ask, "Where is Ron Paul"

The Strasbourg Tea Party - Europe for Ron Paul

http://www.youtube.com/watch?v=07TVBLFroSM

Europe has very active and passionate Ron Paul supporters. They've been struggling with the problems caused by excessive government limiting freedom for longer than people in the USA. The freedom message has a deeper meaning to people in Europe.

Ron Paul, the Rock Star

The 5th Republican debate was held in Dearborn Michigan. Just like any place Ron Paul goes crowds of people show up to support him. To a certain degree, the national campaign was unaware of how much support Ron Paul really had because none of the staff knew how to measure Evangelism Marketing campaigns.

A few people in the national campaign had seen the video of the Air Plane flying over U of M stadium for the Notre Dame game. The staff planned to have Ron Paul speak at the Dearborn campus of U of M after the debate. U of M Dearborn is a commuter campus. Very few attend the Dearborn campus and no one lives there. Fortunately we convinced them to go to a rally in Ann Arbor instead.

I had just flown back from Paris. The front page news in Europe was the collapsing value of the dollar. During the two weeks I was in Paris the dollar lost 9.73% of its value. When I asked the politicians and special guests leaving the debates in Dearborn about the collapsing value of the dollar none of them knew what I was talking about.

I finished up in Dearborn and rushed to Ann Arbor. When I got there I knew something was unusual. Having grown up and attended graduate school there I had tons of secret free parking places. All of my places to park were full. I had to pay to park in the structure. As I drove through town I saw a woman walking with a Ron Paul sign. That is when I knew this was big. I parked my car, grabbed my camera and ran to the Diag where the rally was taking place.

Ron Paul U of M Rally Michigan Part 1

http://www.youtube.com/watch?v=i-71lwDWRf8

As I approached the graduate library I saw the crowd, it was amazing. People were everywhere, it was the kind of thing you expect for a rock star. Thousand's of people filling the plaza at the graduate library.

Alex, one of the University of Michigan student coordinators, had a full concert PA and light system running. Music was playing and the audience was shoulder to shoulder far into the distance, Ron Paul signs were everywhere.

This was easily the largest event I ever saw on the Diag. The Detroit Free Press sent a photographer and the local public radio station sent a reporter to record the event but not one TV crew showed up. Fortunately there were a dozen independent professional cameramen videoing the event.

Ron Paul spoke for an hour and talked directly about the Federal Reserve collapsing the value of the dollar and how it was hurting average people while making bankers rich. The crowd shouted in support as a few people lit Federal Reserve Notes on fire in protest. These normal people were cheering for a lecture on macro economic policy. Where the professional politicians at the debate didn't even know what was happening.

The crowd was peaceful and well mannered. After Dr. Paul finished speaking he went out into the crowd and signed autographs and posed for photographs for over an hour.

The next day a Hillary Clinton supporter had an article published in the Michigan Daily, one of two university newspapers, stating he was treated badly.

There were over a dozen cameras there, mine included. I remembered seeing one person in the front holding an anti Ron Paul sign. I looked through the footage and it just so happened that was the guy and he was sitting in front of my camera the entire time. I had a complete video record of everything that happened to him during the rally.

I watched all the footage and the only time anyone talked to him was after he said something to an elderly woman who seemed very offended by what he said. Then I saw something shocking. When the national anthem was played everyone went silent, put down their signs, and turned to face the flag, except for him. During the national anthem of the United States of America he was waving a sign in people's faces that said, "Ron Paul is wrong on Israel." and a statement by Hillary Clinton supporting Israel.

Not only was his claims of ill treatment a lie but they were the exact opposite of the truth and the opinion he was forcing on others was based on false claims.

During the rally itself, Ron Paul said the same thing he has always said about Israel. The USA should stop supporting both sides of the conflict between Israel and Palestine and let them sort it out for themselves. He pointed out the insanity of providing foreign aid to both sides of a military conflict and how the USA had prevented attempts from both sides to achieve a resolution to the conflict.

One of the points Ron Paul makes about Israel is that a small minority is dictating the policy of the overwhelming majority even in clear contradiction to the facts and the law. It was very striking that this one anti-Paul protester was also lying in an attempt to overshadow the love demonstrated by thousands of people.

Illustration 2: Rally University of Michigan Oct 2007

Illustration 3: Paris Ron Paul Meetup in front of Eiffel Tower

Forums,Chats & Streams. Oh My!

There are two Internets. The wires, antennas, computer software, and electronic devices are what most people think of as the Internet. The real Internet is the connections between people. The network of ideas and relationships is the real Internet. The real Internet exists regardless of the technology used.

The power of the Internet is how it amplifies communication. The Internet increases the ability to communicate and the effectiveness of the messages being communicated. All the new technology makes it faster, easier and less

> Community is built on communication. The Internet builds communities.

expensive to communicate in multiple formats. You can quickly share text, pictures, audio and video with people anywhere in the world. People can get a better feeling for each other and what they are saying. They share the connection.

The easier it is for people to share ideas the faster ideas spread. The Internet allows people separated by time and space to join together. The communities are formed through communication. Many web sites are called communities and to a certain degree that is true. But in reality a single web site is more like a tavern or café where people meet and have conversations. The community is broader and based on values, topics of interest and relationships.

The Ron Paul Revolution is a community. Love of freedom is the shared bond that connects the people together. People visit websites and chat rooms and even meet off-line to share their love of freedom. The Internet is the tool to find and communicate with other members of their community. The Internet allows people separated by time and space to unite into a real community of shared principles and goals.

People have been using the Internet to communicate for decades. Long before the world-wide-web was invented people sent e-mail, posted to bulletin boards, and talked live using chat. The pre-web users formed their own community. They explored the undiscovered territory of cyberspace. As time went on they built the infrastructure to create a new society that was distinct from the physical world they whimsically called, "meat space". They called the physical world "meat space" because cyberspace is made of information and people are made of meat.

Cyberspace is free. You can do anything, be anything and go anywhere. The early inhabitants of cyberspace or netizens as they called themselves established rules to organize their vibrant and growing society. They called the rules netiquette.

Netiquette isn't law, it's more of a semi-formal set of guidelines to help people get along. In general, the worst thing you could do is annoy people and the worst punishment was to be banned from the site or chat room. Most of the time netizens politely, or not so politely, point out the offense and simply use the automated ignore features. Individuals were free to choose who and what they wanted to pay attention to for as long as they wanted.

Having an enjoyable community was the only reward needed to encourage people to improve the online places they spent their time. The people with authority, called operators, were volunteers. There wasn't

> ### Basic Netiquette:
>
> 1. Respect everyone online. Do not spread rumors or send hateful or harmful messages. Don't use inappropriate and offensive language.
>
> 2. Think before you type; make sure what you write cannot be misinterpreted. Use emoticons or abbreviations to convey humor, teasing, or other emotions while online.
>
> 3. Avoid spamming. Unwanted junk mail, chain letters, and jokes can be annoying and time consuming.
>
> 4. Use the KISS principle - Keep It Simple Silly. Be short and to the point in both e-mails and in chatrooms.
>
> 5. Don't type in all CAPITAL letters. This is considered shouting by the online community.
>
> 6. Don't be pest and annoy people while online. People may have work to do and can't continue to communicate with you at that particular time.
>
> *Proposed complete guide to netiquette:*
> *http://www.dtcc.edu/cs/rfc1855.html*

any benefit to being an operator, other than having a nice place to share ideas. The only requirement to be an operator was respect and some skill. If the operator didn't keep the place nice then people could easily make another place.

The term "nice" depended on the shared values of the community that hung out there. In some places language was crude and the subject matter was torrid. In other places strict adherence to decorum was a requirement. Since no one was forced to be any one place it all just sorted itself out.

Cyberspace proved that freedom works.

With the overarching sense of cooperation in cyberspace and the new capabilities of the technologies, people were able to accomplish things that were previously the stuff of imagination.

The most commonly known methods of communication on the Internet mirror off-line communication methods. E-mail, blogs, and now Voice Over Internet Protocol (VOIP) telephony share the features of their off-line equivalents. The Internet versions are cheaper, faster, easier to use, and often do things the off-line version can't.

The technologies that don't have equivalent off-line versions create some of the most remarkable results.

Some of the most interesting technologies with the most impact are:

- Chat
- Forums
- Video
- Voice
- Meetup
- Voting
- Graphs

The way the Internet allows people to deal differently with time creates possibilities that were hard to imagine before.

Because its so cheap to store material and its easy to search for older material anyone can catch up on topics. This is great for people just learning a subject. Since everyone alive today and any time in the future can access what you publish its also great for publishers. Of course if you lied it might not be so great.

Always being able to go back and check on information is helpful for getting facts straight and most efficiently using your time. We call accessing previously released information "time shifting". You shift the time when you see it from when it was first published. This isn't all that unusual for printed material but for broadcast audio and video it makes a huge difference. Time shifting stretches the life of information and expands the audience.

The Internet also allows time compression. When you talk on the phone to someone, long silent pauses feel uncomfortable. You are left waiting and wondering. Is the other person going to say anything else? Are they gone? Can I talk now?

Chat

The Internet allows a very different form of communication called chat. In chat you type back and forth. One of the beauties of chat is you don't have to wait for the other person to stop talking for you to say something else. Plus you can look back at what was said to reinterpret or catch up on something you might have missed.

When you learn to chat you realize you can read and write at the same time. Its possible to hold multiple conversations at once. And since you can scroll back to catch things you missed you can do something else for a moment without much problem.

Chat is fast.

There are two types of Internet chat, instant messenger and chat rooms. Instant messenger is person to person similar to a telephone call. Several of the chat programs also allow voice and video. They also feature conferencing as well. Additionally, you can send files to each other. This makes it easy for people to collaborate on projects. These programs are good for contacting people you already know. Some of the programs are Yahoo Messenger, ICQ, and Skype. Skype is primarily focused on voice calling but it has a chat feature as well.

People all over the world are staying in touch and even building their relationships using chat technology. I personally have friends in France, Texas, Panama, and Thailand who I chat with regularly. Every time I log on to the Internet I look to see if they are online or if they sent a message while I was offline. I've met new business partners, founded companies, and conducted business all through chat and never met the partners or customers in person.

The second type of chat is chat rooms. These are a way for many people to meet and talk. Chat rooms are very much like a tavern or café. You can see how people talk and treat others and get to know their inside without the misleading facade of the outside. Intelligence and creativity outweigh the superficial status symbols of "meat space".

Chat rooms are organized by subjects of conversation and stay open as long as someone is there to talk. IRC is the oldest, most established form of chat rooms. Chat rooms predated instant messengers.

Chat overcomes many of the social norms that slow down conversations in the off-line world. Some of the behaviors considered polite in "meat space" don't apply in cyberspace. If you want to talk about a certain topic just start talking. If anyone else is interested they will respond. If others aren't interested they will ignore you. If you are annoying, they will just have their computers filter what you say out. Unless you are trying to annoy people it doesn't happen very often since there are sites and chat rooms for every topic. You can easily find people to share your interests.

You can have your computer highlight certain words so you can quickly see items of most interest to you and jump in on those topics. People most often use this feature to keep track of messages directed to them by name. This is like a continuously running Google of the conversation. These filter features allow you to easily pay attention to far more information than you could in normal life.

If you've never been in a good chat room, imagine 20-100 people simultaneously talking about 3-10 topics and everyone being able to pay attention to all of it. That is chat.

> ..imagine 20-100 people simultaneously talking about 3-10 topics and everyone being able to pay attention to all of it.

Chat isn't just public, you can have private chats as well. This allows you to switch focus between multiple conversations with one or more people. Because it feels comfortable to wait for someone to respond you can keep up with more chats at once than talking in person or on the phone. And you can do other work on the computer at the same time.

The hyper-speed of this type of communication allows Ron Paul supporters to discover, discuss and plan projects 10 to 100 times as fast as would be possible meeting face to face. People from all over the world 24-hours a day can contribute to the revolution.

Many people who got fed up with the taxes, excessive regulation and villainy committed in their name left the United States. These people tend to be among the best and the brightest. In the old world, they would have been removed from American politics. With the Internet, these people are able to participate and contribute ideas and money.

The Ron Paul Revolution is running 24 hours a day and moves very fast. While the professional campaigners are sleeping, the creative and dedicated Ron Paul supporters all over the world are busy.

Cell phones offer a different form of fast text conversations called SMS, short message system. SMS is similar to e-mail but only for short messages and it is delivered to your cell phone. Many of the Instant Messenger systems can also send SMS.

SMS doesn't demand the same dedicated attention as a telephone call. You can receive a message and read it when you get a moment. Kids often use SMS to talk in class without interrupting the rest of the class. They set their cell phones on vibrate and hold entire conversations without missing a beat. Because SMS is text it also works in places that are too loud to receive a phone call like a night club. Groups of friends all over town update each other about where the best party is happening and meet at the hot spot.

SMS allows groups to plan and organize their activities on the fly. Some groups of Ron Paul supporters use SMS to notify their members of events making it possible to get groups to show up quickly when needed.

Forums

Blogs receive a lot of attention in the traditional media. Probably because blogs closely resemble a newspaper or magazine. Because blogs resemble newspapers, the traditional media seems to understand the concept. One feature that many traditional media outlets don't understand is comments. The Internet is a two-way communication system. Your audience can talk back. But more than talk back they can build upon your posts and expand the conversation spreading it to new people.

Most forum software has threaded posts. Threaded means the conversations are linked making it easy to follow from beginning through all the evolution to all the branches the conversation takes. If you discover a conversation late into the development you can easily trace it back to see what led to where it is now.

The tens of thousand's of Ron Paul supporters read all the sources of information and talk back. Every post about Ron Paul quickly receives a large number of comments. The people that oppose Ron Paul claim these are SPAM. While they might be unwanted by the poster, they aren't the result of robots. Its easy to see from the unique names, the different IP addresses (the unique ID of your computer connection), and the relevancy of the comments that its a whole lot of real people.

Red State, a conservative forum, got annoyed with all the new people joining to talk about Ron Paul. Red State banned posts and comments about Ron Paul from anyone who had not been a member for over 6 months.

The actions of Red State seemed very odd on the Internet. Free speech is the norm on the Internet. Its very easy to filter out SPAM. This wasn't SPAM. This was legitimate posts of people that seriously support the only real

> Red State violated the Law of Unintended Consequences.

conservative presidential candidate. Red State censored rather than filtered and that offends a lot of netizens, even those that don't support Ron Paul.

The result of their totalitarian short sightedness was a ton of bad press for Red State and more supporters for Ron Paul. They broke one of the natural laws. The law of unintended consequences states that when you initiate force you get unintended consequences that, ironically, often turn out to be the exact opposite of what you planned.

Red State should have added a Ron Paul section to their web site then moved posts to that area. This would have kept the strictly Ron Paul posts from cluttering up the rest of their forum and allowed more real discussion of topics. The heavy handed way Red State acted was similar to the way the old politicians operate in "meat space". They stuck their head in the sand and punished anyone that questions their fantasy.

The reason Red State acted the way they did is because they were trying to keep their readers from discovering Ron Paul. Cyberspace is a world of information. The entire existence of cyberspace is sharing ideas. People discuss freely and decide for themselves. The best ideas win.

> "Information wants to be free".
> -- Stewart Brand

Politics is about power and control. Fortunately for lovers of freedom, information is immune from power and usually finds a way around control.

Information wants to be free. This observation about how information seems to always find a way to spread is one of the most important aspects to understand about cyberspace and Evangelism Marketing.

You can put chains on information but the only way to kill an idea is to kill everyone that knows the idea and every record it existed. But even trying such draconian tactics will not destroy the idea. Anyone can have the same idea again, and then, it springs back to life looking to spread.

Red State is just one forum in a giant see of forums on the Internet. When Ron Paul announced his web site, it left a lot to be desired. But geeks love Ron Paul so almost immediately people were putting up forums to allow each other to share information on Ron Paul.

RonPaulForurms.com is one of the largest most influential forums. RonPaulForums.com was created by supporters acting completely independently of the national campaign. If Ron Paul's, staff had been better informed about the Internet they would have created a forum right on the official campaign site, RonPaul2008.com. Because they didn't create a forum on the official site a bunch of other volunteer sites sprang up and divided the community. DailyPaul is another site like RonPaulForums that gained a lot of popularity and became a hub for supporters to find information. If Ron Paul's staff had created a forum on the official site it would have allowed information to freely flow to and from the campaign. Getting the traffic to go to a central place makes it much easier to judge how much traffic you have, where its coming from, and what the visitors want to see.

As late as October the RonPaul2008.com web site was not using any type of server statistics to track visitors. There is no excuse for that since Google offers free tools that can be implemented in minutes. Actually, most community tools are free and can be implemented in minutes. The Open Source community has been sharing all these tools for years.

RonPaulForums became a central place to share information. As more people shared information there, more people came there to share even more information. The large amount of Ron Paul specific traffic to the site made it possible to launch big events like the money bombs. Anyone that was interested in donating time or money could look on Ron Paul Forums for a project to participate in.

As more information was published and links posted from one web site to another Ron Paul sites grew in ranking on Google. The more posts and the more links the easier it was for more and more people to find out about Ron Paul. It just snowballs. Exponential growth is the nature of information and Evangelism Marketing.

Video

The entire chapter, "The Revolution Will Not Be Televised" covers the use of video in promoting the message of Ron Paul so I will only cover a few key points in this section.

Video is now so easy to share that many people posted videos when web page posts might have expressed the message better with text on a website. Since YouTube is so popular, posting a video is likely to get more views faster than an ordinary website. Watching a video on YouTube also gives you a list of other related videos. You can keep clicking from one video to the next and dozens of videos on the topic you like. More importantly, you can find interesting connections between topics. These connections open up entirely new communities to share the Ron Paul Revolution.

Voice

Telephones have been around for nearly 100 years and nearly everyone has a telephone. Even children have cell phones these days. Voice over the Internet in the form of streaming radio or downloaded audio files like MP3s has been around for 10 years. Combining the improved capabilities of audio on the Internet and computers handling phone calls provides extremely powerful tools for promoting Ron Paul.

One of the more creative uses of voice technology I saw was Freedom Message. Most people hate reaching a machine on the telephone but one Ron Paul supporter turned a voice mail system into a fabulous tool to promote Ron Paul.

Freedom Message is a phone number with voice mail boxes that each play a different 2-5 minute long recording of Ron Paul talking about an issue. Freedom Message has printed cards with the phone numbers to call to hear the messages. When you meet someone who is interested in Ron Paul you can hand them a card and let them listen for themselves. This makes it very easy for even the most shy supporter to spread the message. It is a great way to help people who aren't on the Internet hear Ron Paul in his own words. Very powerful!

Another very quick and easy voice technique a bunch of people used was to include a Ron Paul message on their personal voice mail. Every time someone left a voice mail they first heard a message promoting Ron Paul.

I also heard of people asking telemarketers who called them and operators at call centers if they would vote for Ron Paul. The operators were glad to hear something positive. Many times it would lead to a favorable response for Ron Paul.

Meetup

Meetup is a web site that allows people to find others in their geographical area who share the same interests. Using the web site they schedule a time and place to "meet up." The "Get Involved" link on the official Ron Paul campaign

directed supporters to Meetup.com. This was good in the beginning but caused a ton of problems as the Revolution grew.

Meetup is focused on local groups. It doesn't work very well for a large movement spread over the entire world. The Howard Dean campaign used Meetup. The myth among the politicians was the Howard Dean campaign used the Internet very well. The political staffers don't understand the Internet and they definitely don't understand the depth of breadth of Ron Paul's support. The political staffers just copied the Howard Dean campaign thinking that was how to be successful.

Meetup doesn't have a convenient way for groups to share information. There is no way through Meetup to send an e-mail to all the Ron Paul groups at once. This meant people had to join several groups and relay messages from one group to another. Also, Meetup charges each group $15 per month to use the service. RonPaul2008 could have had a much better system and offer it for free to volunteers saving hundreds of thousand's of dollars.

Voting

Ron Paul has won every online poll. When his supporters see a poll, they tell all their friends. One of the supporter web sites stopped posting links to the polls and instead required visitors to copy and paste the URL into their browser manually. The reason they did this was to keep votes from being censored. Its very easy to censor all the votes coming from a certain site. A blog that is critical of Ron Paul claimed this was a way to inflate votes. That is exactly the opposite. Not posting links and requiring manual action stops spiders and other robots. Every vote coming from that Ron Paul site was a person who was motivated enough to type the URL for the poll in by hand.

Many of the big corporate media and Republican party web sites just stopped providing Ron Paul on the list of candidates. In one case they listed Brownbeck after he had already dropped out but they refused to list Ron Paul. Ron Paul supporters voted for Brownbeck in that poll and listed their e-mail address as RonPaul2008 to protest the obvious attempt to manipulate the results.

Judging from how much supporters of other candidates complain about Ron Paul supporters "spamming" polls its making an impression. Its really very funny to see the editorial commentary on a site describing Ron Paul as a long shot and the sites very own poll shows him winning by double digits.

Polls don't spread the message but they do increase name recognition and show others Ron Paul can win.

Charts

Evangelism Marketing is all about information. The better the information the more it spreads and the more it spreads the faster it spreads. Supporters like to know their work is making a difference. Ron Paul Graphs made a huge difference in showing people the progress.

The distributed nature of an Evangelism Marketing campaign makes it hard to know what is happening. RonPaulGraphs.com gathered information from many sources and published a whole host of up to date graphs showing the progress of the Ron Paul Revolution. Some of the graphs are even updated live.

RonPaulGraphs.com acted all on their own and provided a great service during the money bombs by allowing supporters to track the progress without causing excess traffic to the main campaign site that might prevent donations.

RonPaulGraphs.com makes the election an open and transparent process. It would be great to see the same amount of transparency in government.

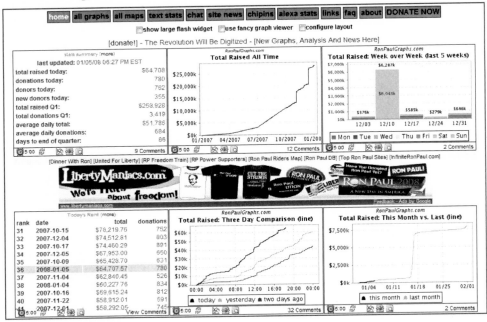

Paul My Ride

Americans have a love affair with their cars. Customizing cars is a major industry. Combine the love of cars with the love of freedom and you get some creative Ron Paul rides.

http://www.youtube.com/watch?v=gLMEKDqugHc

In Michigan people like to get outside. Between rain in the summer and snow in the winter, the last thing you want to do when the weather is good is ask people to stay inside to watch a political video. But Michigan is also home of Detroit, The Motor City. If you can do something cool with a vehicle you can get a crowd.

So if you can't get people to watch videos at home bring the videos to them. A Jackson County, Michigan supporter did some creative engineering and mounted a 53" Plasma Screen TV and DVD player in the bed of his truck. The Ron Paul TV Truck was a big hit where ever he took it.

Reynolds Kosloskey, another Michigan resident, was apathetic about politics and politicians. When he discovered Ron Paul his apathy was cured. He was so enthused he had to show the world how much he wanted

http://www.youtube.com/watch?v=nppzm05c6q0

Ron Paul for president. He started with bumper stickers, but that wasn't enough. So he made his own 4 foot by 2 foot stickers for the side of his truck. He then decided that was just not enough either. So he built a frame for the bed of his truck to carry three 8 foot long 4 foot high Ron Paul signs that he created himself.

Not only did he do this, he photographed the entire project and produced a very well made how-to video showing anyone how to do the same.

Image 34: Granny Warrior's RV

Some of the most unlikely people get in on the act when it comes to promoting Ron Paul. A couple of retired old women calling themselves The Granny Warriors painted up their Recreational Vehicle and went on the road to promote Ron Paul and Freedom.

The list of vehicles customized to promote Ron Paul goes on and on. There are vans in New York, cars in Florida, and even a few airplanes. Of course, don't forget the Ron Paul Blimp.

Image 35: Ron Paul Blimp   http://www.ronpaulblimp.com/

Sing His Praises

In the beginning I thought about helping promote awareness of Ron Paul by getting a song written by a well known artist.

Peter Keys plays keyboard for Parliament Funkadelic, and has toured with Bob Segar & Kid Rock. I met Peter when he worked for me on the Bikini Calculus DVD. That experiment in Viral Marketing resulted in one of the Top 100 Most Popular Viral Videos of All Times and validated all my theoretical models. So I knew I could get a lot of attention.

Since Peter is a big advocate of individual freedom he quickly agreed to donate a song to help the Ron Paul campaign. We made plans to use a song from his new band, See Peoples.

Before we could even get started on the project dozens of other bands released songs for Ron Paul including:

- Poker Face - www.youtube.com/watch?v=Dy4P2KZI-eM
- Knights of Liberty - www.youtube.com/watch?v=AlPjsGFcXlg
- The Violets - www.youtube.com/watch?v=L-t_YD-sDhw
- Three Shoe Posse - www.youtube.com/watch?v=naMtwqBzja0
- King Solomon - www.youtube.com/watch?v=-bCRc2ub8hU
- Aimee Allen - www.aimeeallen.com

After seeing how many fabulous songs were being written I decided my efforts could be better applied in other ways. One of those ways was producing videos. And I did end up using a song from The Violets for the music video I hand delivered to Ron Paul.

As of Dec 1, 2007 there are over 160 songs written for Ron Paul. Bands write Ron Paul songs just so they will get more attention for themselves. Ron Paul doesn't just have rock star popularity, he makes rocks stars popular.

The collection of Ron Paul music is as varied as his supporters. There is pop, hard rock, rap, country, folk, reggae, and even a Frank Sinatra impersonator doing a Ron Paul version of "New York, New York". Ron Paul doesn't only bring people together politically, he brings them together musically.

The Violets Music Video

www.youtube.com/watch?v=L-t_YD-sDhw

An up an coming band promoted themselves by promoting Ron Paul in this energetic and uplifting song and appealing video.

Poker Face Music Video

www.youtube.com/watch?v=FFW0siFFOCA

Poker Face has been putting out freedom oriented music for a long time. They are serious about freedom. This song addresses some hard hitting issues while promoting Ron Paul.

Knights of Liberty Music Video

www.youtube.com/watch?v=AlPjsGFcXlg

www.myspace.com/knightsofliberty

Knights of Liberty are a rap duo who present Ron Paul's message in a very effective way with catchy rhymes, melodies and rhythms.

"If you don't want the state taking food off your plate then vote for Ron Paul in 2008"

Three Shoe Posse

www.youtube.com/watch?v=naMtwqBzja0

Ron Paul Is Here, by Three Shoe Posse was on of the first Ron Paul songs. Like others to come the reggae song provided a lot of information about Ron Paul's comprehensive message and did it with a very catchy tune.

Herding Cats

On the surface its a very strange collection of people that support Ron Paul. Every race, religion, life style, and economic status support Ron Paul. These people have very little in common in their everyday lives but they do agree on the message of freedom.

Having such a varied group makes things difficult at times. The specific issues hold different significance to each person and those don't often translate to the mass market in the way most people think. Its very personal. You will find your own reason for loving Ron Paul. Veterans of World War II who value second amendment rights don't usually talk to pot smoking anarchists who don't hang out with middle class mothers from the suburbs. But they really do share something in common. They all want to live their lives in peace, free from government harassment and be able to afford to buy the things they need.

The freedom message really does bring people together. This is great but also confusing. Even though the message is shared by many people it took someone with an absolutely perfect track record of honesty and integrity to motivate people.

Democrats & Republicans have claimed to be for freedom or peace or lower taxes or improving the economy but those were empty campaign promises. Ron Paul's message isn't a bunch of fluff. He explains why things aren't going right and how to fix it. He lays out the entire plan. Equally important, Ron Paul has kept his word even when it was unpopular. People trust Ron Paul. That trust is why he is the lightening rod for the freedom movement.

Other campaigns are better organized and even provide fabulous Internet tools to help their supporters. But it hasn't done much for them. You must have a message people believe. People don't spend their time, money and risk their reputation on lies or promises that will never be kept.

Barack Obama has the most support of all the other candidates and probably has the most grassroots support of the other candidates. A quick look through any city, even a college town and you'll notice the only bumper stickers or signs you see are for Ron Paul. Not only doesn't Obama have as many supporters, they aren't as dedicated.

After the November 5th money bomb, an Obama supporter tried to have a money bomb for Obama. It was posted on Obama's web site and reported on Wired.com. They said, "If a bunch of crazy people can raise $5 million in a day for Ron Paul, we should be able to do the same for Obama," When the time came only 72 people contributed for a total of $4,650. It was embarrassing and the media never mentioned it again.

http://blog.wired.com/27bstroke6/2007/11/in-role-reversa.html

Barack's Friday

http://my.barackobama.com/page/group/BaracksFridayNovthe16th

Mike Huckabee also tried to get his supporters to copy Ron Paul's supporters but failed. The fact they were trying to copy Ron Paul showed Ron Paul is the leader. But more significant than the now glaringly obvious greater support for Ron Paul was that the Money Bomb was spontaneous. Ron Paul didn't organize it, supporters did. And it wasn't one supporter trying to get others to follow, as was the case of Obama. A large group of Ron Paul supporters passed around the idea then came to an agreement. It was the shared idea.

Recognizing free people can choose how they will spend their time and money and might not agree with you is the first step in encouraging an Evangelism Marketing campaign. You can't manage or direct people that are doing what they want because they want to do it. All you can do is share really good ideas and let them decide to join you.

The skill levels among the volunteers range from none to top experts in every field needed for success. One of the skills most lacking amongst volunteers was simple salesmanship. They didn't know how to talk to people in a non-offensive way that motivated action.

Promoting Ron Paul is extremely easy but having a good approach can double, triple or even quadruple your effectiveness. Several very talented people shared their knowledge with others to raise the expertise of all supporters.

I co-hosted several shows on Ron Paul Radio to answer questions from the audience and demonstrate techniques with the other host. Craig Rowland, another supporter created a great series of videos and published them on YouTube. His instructional videos helped people overcome their reluctance to talk to strangers by giving them easy to use techniques to succeed in spreading the message of Liberty. His videos also raised the effectiveness of people that were already good at promoting Ron Paul.

Bringing 60,000 people up to speed within weeks would have been impossible without tools like the videos Craig Rowland created and posted on YouTube for all the supporters to watch.

Image 36: Liberty Sells itself Instructional Video
http://www.youtube.com/watch?v=gr3yEvGOAi8
http://www.youtube.com/watch?v=Ra4vksazLec
http://www.youtube.com/watch?v=9LOyn-vwfVl

November 5th Money Bomb Promo

http://www.youtube.com/watch?v=yh_9fip694A

A video posted on YouTube to encourage people to contribute to Ron Paul on November 5th, 2007, the date of the first money bomb.

Ron Paul Blimp Promo

http://www.youtube.com/watch?v=W6l5zYu541Q

Ron Paul Blimp on CNN after the money was raised

http://www.youtube.com/watch?v=W6l5zYu541Q

The primary goal of the blimp was to do something so big that it created buzz in the media. It got some attention but probably not as much as could have been achieved with the same amount of money.

Joey Pencil, Ron Paul Video

http://www.youtube.com/watch?v=PE77ooE5_Eo

Lots of professionals donate their time to support Ron Paul. Joey Pencil created this TV ad and gave it away. As always, the national campaign didn't use it.

Pennsylvania Dec 10, 2007 Rally

Part 1 http://www.youtube.com/watch?v=8RqJZ06KeX0

Part 2 http://www.youtube.com/watch?v=upYV9RxIjfM

Part 3 http://www.youtube.com/watch?v=D8-_O2rWZJA

Part 4 http://www.youtube.com/watch?v=GVNDAvxfG7l

Part 5 http://www.youtube.com/watch?v=r_yS2Hm_0AQ

Something Big Commercial

http://www.youtube.com/watch?v=wPjTAH8Y_L8

CNN asked each candidate to choose a video submitted by users of YouTube for a special spot on the televised debate. The video selected by the Ron Paul campaign included footage from one of the guys working with me on the Ann Arbor Rally. I watched this debate with the leaders of the Washtenaw County Republicans. It was a bit shocking for the Ron Paul supporters and the other Republicans watching with me to see my footage on TV.

Can't Buy Me Love

One of the biggest complaints about American presidential politics is how much money is needed to win. Fund raising has become the way people judge the success of candidates. Advertising on national TV costs millions of dollars. However, advertising isn't where most of the money is spent. Most of the money is spent on salaries, office space, travel, fund raising and other overhead.

Candidate	Overhead %	Overhead $
John McCain	80.37%	22,764,266
Barack Obama	77.96%	34,167,912
Rudolph Giuliani	77.49%	23,374,686
Hillary Clinton	76.67%	31,017,863
Fred Thompson	73.75%	4,207,679
Mitt Romney	56.50%	30,285,855
Ron Paul	54.07%	1,830,065

Table 2: Campaign Overhead % By Candidate.
Note: Mitt Romney's classified $10,981,902 as Miscellaneous Media and $17 million of his contributions was his own money.

By the third quarter the establishment candidates spent on average $28,322,116 on overhead. Ron Paul by contrast spent 54.07% directly on reaching supporters. And since Ron Paul's total overhead was only $1,830,065 he likely had a higher percentage of fixed costs then the other candidates which reduced his efficiency.

If you are spending tens of millions of dollars the only people able to compete are either billionaires willing to spend their own money or long time insiders bought and paid for by special interest groups who expect to be repaid with pork barrel handouts when the candidates they fund are elected. 70% to 80% of the money isn't even spent campaigning. It goes into salaries, luxury hotels, expensive meals, and rental of high priced office space.

The system is so corrupted that special interests and corporations often contribute to candidates on both sides just to guarantee access later on.

	Hillary Clinton (D)	Barack Obama (D)	Rudolph Giuliani (R)	Mitt Romney (R)	John McCain (R)
Bear Stearns	$120,580		$147,691		
Citigroup Inc	$307,350	$180,650	$137,350	$94,150	$137,050
Credit Suisse Group		$92,300	$164,900	$66,850	$58,950
Goldman Sachs	$350,050	$369,078	$79,750	$181,425	$88,700
JP Morgan Chase & Co	$173,350	$216,759	$71,200	$67,450	$59,850
Lehman Brothers	$123,450	$229,090	$140,850	$60,750	$53,250
Merrill Lynch	$125,550		$151,000	$147,200	$113,575
Morgan Stanley	$323,550	$104,425	$97,950	$110,050	$50,950
Wall Street Money	**$1,523,880**	**$1,192,302**	**$990,691**	**$727,875**	**$562,325**

Table 3: Top Contributors to Establishment Candidates. Source: OpenSecrets.org

You can see for yourself who is contributing to which campaigns at www.OpenSecrets.org. The establishment candidates top contributors are employees of Wall Street bankers and brokerage houses.

The average annual bonus for all Goldman Sach's employees is $360,000. The CEO received a bonus of $67.9 million in 2007.

http://www.marketwatch.com/News/Story/Story.aspx?guid=%7BE1669880-AE13-42FA-BDD0-292655C7710B%7D

The people that benefit from the inflation caused by the Federal Reserve creating money are the ones contributing the most to the campaigns of the establishment politicians.

Contributions to Hillary Clinton	
Cablevision Systems	$135,113
News Corp	$99,350
Time Warner	$124,150
Total	**$358,613**

Table 4: Media Contributors to Hillary Clinton. Source: OpenSecrets.org

The establishment candidates also receive huge undeclared contributions from the big media in the form of free favorable news coverage. As of Q3 Hillary Clinton only spent $99,874 on broadcast media and Rudolph Giuliani spent a minuscule $2,004.

The amount of money Hillary Clinton spent didn't even match the amount of contributions received from employees of the big media corporations. It's interesting to note that employees of Ruppert Murdoch's company, News Corp who owns the supposedly conservative Fox News network, are among the top contributors to Hillary Clinton.

These companies all have a vested interest in favorable government treatment. They rely on licenses and rules that restrict competition.

Aside from the financiers, attorneys and accountants are the other top contributors. Attorneys benefit from all the regulations created by politicians. Increased prosecutions and lawsuits subsidize lawyers through increased billable hours. The majority of the work done by accountants is to satisfy mandated reporting or to minimize the impact of taxes. Both attorneys and accountants benefit greatly from the laws and taxes instituted by the government officials they help elect.

Conventional wisdom says that a principled candidate who consistently votes against spending tax payers money on pork barrel handouts has no chance. That makes Ron Paul look like a joke to political insiders and establishment media.

Before Ron Paul even had materials for volunteers to distribute they were out spreading the word, making signs and posting videos and articles on the Internet.

McCain is nearly out of money. Ron Paul has more money on hand than all the other Republicans except Giuliani. While Giuliani's polls and Google search statistics are steadily declining. Ron Paul's support is growing exponentially.

Ron Paul is getting his money a little bit at a time from tens of thousands of regular people. Ron Paul gets more money from active duty military than any of the other candidates. Soldiers in the US Air Force, US Army, and US Navy rank among the highest sources of contributions to Ron Paul's campaign. From personally speaking with active duty soldiers its clear why they support Ron Paul. In the words of a US Marine I met in an airport who had returned from Iraq, "We will follow orders because that is what we are trained to do but the war is not working and we don't want to be over there."

Image 37: Ron Paul #1 with the Military

People contribute their time and money where it most benefits their lives. Soldiers don't want to die on foreign shores. That is strong motivation to support Ron Paul who is the only candidate who both voted against the military invasion before it started and will bring the troops home immediately. The other supposed leading candidate's won't commit to ever removing all our troops.

Soldiers clearly aren't apposed to fighting to defend the nation. They willingly put their lives at risk when needed to protect our nation. Soldiers like Ron Paul's wise advice to follow the Constitution and use the appropriate amount and type of force. They would prefer to either declare war, fight it, win it and come home or defend our own borders and use Letters of Marque and Reprisal to deal with international criminals.

Ron Paul is the #1 candidate on the Internet. He so overwhelms the other candidates, they claim his apparent massive support isn't real but only the work of a small group of spammers. There are companies you can hire to strategically place links to your web site in blogs and online communities. And we all know about the e-mail spam promoting certain products. Is it possible Ron Paul hired one of those companies? Lets look at the finances to see how well buying Internet support works.

Candidate	Internet Media	% of Average
John McCain	$2,550,969	251.26%
Hillary Clinton	$1,140,350	112.32%
Fred Thompson	$948,253	93.40%
Mitt Romney	$918,943	90.51%
Rudolph Giuliani	$731,197	72.02%
Barack Obama	$693,753	68.33%
Ron Paul	$123,403	12.15%
Average	$1,015,267	

Table 5: Candidates Internet Spending

If Ron Paul had paid for Internet support, he got a fabulous deal. Ron Paul has only spent 12.05% as much as the average. Hillary Clinton spent 10 times as much and John McCain spent 25 times as much money on the Internet as Ron Paul.

At $123,403 its likely the only money Ron Paul spent was on building his web site and paying for the huge amount of traffic it receives.

The Internet is, for the most part, a free speech zone. Free from censorship and free to publish your message. The long tail filled with millions of people that were filtered out of traditional broadcast media now have a way to be heard.

There isn't some central power filtering what is said on the Internet. The audience decides what is read, seen and heard. They either ignore the stuff they don't like or post rebuttals. Wonkette.com is a blog who's publisher purposely posts articles antagonistic to Ron Paul supporters who she calls "Paultards" because it drastically increases her traffic and thus advertising revenue. Her off based attacks had unintended consequences. When she ridiculed the Ron Paul Blimp she sparked the final surge of money needed to rent the Ron Paul Blimp.

People that are passionate about a message, post to the Internet for free. These passionate people post because they want what they say to be read and seen by as many people as possible.

Employees that post for money aren't as passionate as true supporters. At some point, the work of posting outweighs the reward of the money. The paid employee reaches a point when they rather spend the money they make doing things they love than work any harder.

Ron Paul supporters are passionate about spreading the freedom message. They spend their money so they can spread the message. If they could, they would spend all their time promoting Ron Paul and the freedom message. Numerous people have quit their jobs or come out of retirement just to have more time to dedicate to promoting Ron Paul.

Ron Paul has more people supporting him than any campaign could possibly hire. His supporters work harder than paid employees ever would. Evangelism Marketing is the best campaign finance reform.

Image 38: World Largest Campaign Sign

Lighted Roof Top Sign

http://www.youtube.com/watch?v=9Fv1B8hnfrU

Creative supporter designs his own low cost roof top sign similar to those you see for pizza delivery cars.

Christmas Lights Signs

http://www.youtube.com/watch?v=m8gtr24Z9hl

Instructional video on how to make this totally awesome Ron Paul Christmas Lights sign! Go to http://ronpaul.meetup.com/7/files/ for files needed to make the sign

Ron Paul Revolution, Memphis Style

http://video.google.com/videoplay?docid=919656380013930220

30 People in Memphis Tennessee make news by painting the town Paul. In one night they posted 95 banners and 150 signs all over Memphis.

Roof in New York

www.youtube.com/watch?v=VPYEYzQHcDE

Group in New York painted Google Ron Paul on the roof of their building which is on the flight path for the international airport. The roof top is clearly visible by every flight arriving or departing and the satellite image available on Google Earth and Google Maps.

Ron Paul Has Already Won

The Ron Paul Revolution isn't about politics. It's a way of life. Freedom to live your own life and keep the fruits of your labor to use or give away as you wish without harassment from anyone, especially government. When I see what the supporters have accomplished I'm inspired. I don't think the supporters really understand just what is happening. They are creating a new society here and now.

People who thought they were alone can discover there are thousands and even millions who share their ideas. These like minded people can get together and make their desires reality.

Cyberspace demonstrated that freedom works. The freedom experiment in cyberspace is reaching into the physical world. Developments in technology are empowering distributed action and expansion of freedom.

Tools of all sorts, but particularly computers, are making it easier and cheaper for people to design, manufacture and distribute products and services. Individuals now outsource complex manufacturing to service providers able to handle custom orders for prices competitive to mass production. This book itself is an example of made to order manufacturing. All I needed to do was send the digital file to the publisher and they print as many copies as I want. The same type of services exist for everything from t-shirts to machine tools.

Beyond small run made to order manufacturing, individuals can now afford computer aided manufacturing called 3D printing. This technology makes physical objects as easy to copy as digital information objects.

If people can simply print products, the long tail will extend beyond sight. Everyone can have exactly what they want. If you can't download a design then make one yourself. This distributes power all the way to the individual.

As people can choose exactly what they want when they want where they want in more and more ways it will become harder for governments to lump people into groups. Its already become obvious to most people that they don't identify with a group. Unrestrained individuality is easier than ever before. The ease of communication means being an individual doesn't mean being alone.

The Ron Paul Revolution is just the tip of a much larger shift in the world.

People everywhere are seeing the value of freedom.

People in Europe are encouraging us, their brothers and sisters in the United States. This proves the message is taking hold. They are staging rallies to support us. The Europeans want the Ron Paul Revolution to take hold in their countries. Even though they don't have the man they have the idea. They see the big picture, the long term goal.

Just the fact they are helping us proves the Ron Paul Revolution already won. It might be a long time before the institutions change to match reality. It is possible that things could get a lot worse before they get better. The way free people quickly adapt and work around all the barriers is very encouraging. I believe the same people and techniques needed to get the Ron Paul Revolution to international prominence will help us get through any turmoil caused by those who want to prevent the transition.

Technology is improving exponentially. Communication is increasing exponentially. What visionaries had predicted and we all suspected is now coming true.

We don't need a new government. We don't even need a new leader. All we need is our creativity and ability to communicate and we will build a peaceful, prosperous and free society.

The Ron Paul Revolution is just beginning...

Links

This list of links is to help you get started understanding what is behind The Ron Paul Revolution. I've tried to provide a bit of extra perspective for each link to help you connect events and ideas. Use these links as jumping off points. When you visits sites click on other links. Surf around and see where it leads you. The web is constantly changing and growing. If you discover yourself wanting to promote freedom then post your own material. And please come to the web page for the book and share the links. Keep the revolution growing.

www.RonPaulRevolutionHistoryInTheMaking.com

Vicente Fox Admits to Amero

http://www.youtube.com/watch?v=gYGrn0hZlCQ

One of the issues that opponents ridicule Ron Paul supporters about is the currency planned to replace the individual currencies of the USA, Canada & Mexico with a single North American currency similar to the Euro. This currency will be called the Amero. Critics claim the Amero is conspiracy theory non-sense. Watch former President of Mexico, Vicente Fox, talk about the planned schedule for instituting the Amero.

George Stephanopoulos

http://www.youtube.com/watch?v=fk60hAzwWO4

At the end of a lengthy interview of Ron Paul, former Bill Clinton staffer turned television host, George Stephanopoulos asks Ron Paul what he views as success for his campaign. Ron says, "to win". George shoots back, "You won't win."

Stephanopoulos upgrades Ron Paul - says he's a "Dark Horse"!

http://www.youtube.com/watch?v=e5H8bKpk6MU

After Ron Paul supporters set the record for fund raising Stephanopoulos changes his tune about betting everything he has that Ron Paul won't win. Oddly enough the video clip they used shows me at 0:45.

San Francisco Straw Poll Canceled

www.youtube.com/watch?v=j_GADQv3vKs

San Francisco Republican Party held a dinner to be followed by a straw poll. The dinner cost $33 and included 1 vote in the straw poll. Without dinner it cost $5 to vote in the straw poll. When the straw poll was about to happen and it was clear there were more Ron Paul supporters than other candidates supporters the organizer canceled the poll claiming it was unfair to the people that had paid $33. The Ron Paul supporters immediately agreed to pay the full $33 but were refused.

University of Michigan Rally

Part 1 http://www.youtube.com/watch?v=i-71IwDWRf8

Part 2 http://www.youtube.com/watch?v=eup_HkN3vEg

Part 3 http://www.youtube.com/watch?v=RuiZRzu7khw

Part 4 http://www.youtube.com/watch?v=NONoIEe7LH4

This was a very large rally that almost didn't happen. The national campaign staff were planning on having the rally at the Dearborn campus near where the debate was held. Fortunately, they listened to student organizers at University of Michigan and held the event at the main campus in Ann Arbor where 5,000 people attended.

Michigan State University Tailgate with special guest Mitt Romney

http://www.youtube.com/watch?v=tbg4nPMU088

Mitt Romney and Michigan Republican Chair Saul Anuzis hosted a tailgate party for the MSU vs. UM game. Approximately 25 people attended if you include paid staff and media. Meanwhile over a hundred Ron Paul supporters held a party and had an airplane flying a banner over the stadium supporting Ron Paul.

Student surprising CNN by supporting Ron Paul
http://www.youtube.com/watch?v=6g7xFRjY22s

Apparently CNN expected a Republican to not support Ron Paul. The hosts quickly try minimize Ron Paul's chances of winning and even badger the women into selecting a different candidate. Its striking that the Democrat refused to even name a candidate she would support basically saying "anyone except a Republican". It makes you wonder if she knew Ron Paul was an option.

First Republican Debate
http://www.youtube.com/watch?v=8Hfa7vT02IA

"Bloodbath if we leave Iraq"
http://www.youtube.com/watch?v=av1DjGkORvU

One of the claims frequently used by people promoting the war in Iraq is that if we leave now it will be a blood bath. Ron Paul points out that the same people were claiming the people would love us for invading and it would pay for itself and be completed in a few months.

Morton Downey, Jr.
http://www.youtube.com/watch?v=88REf0tjZHo

Back in the 1980's there was a talk show host that made a name for himself by being verbally abusive and unashamedly stating what he thought was right. Ron Paul appeared on the show during his first run for president as the Libertarian Party nominee. The exchange was very heated but Ron Paul resisted the name calling the practiced by the other people on the show. You can see he hasn't changed his core beliefs.

America: Freedom to Fascism
www.freedomtofascism.com

Aaron Russo, producer of feature films including "Trading Places" starring Eddy Murphy and "The Rose" starring Bette Midler, produced this documentary exposing the truth about the IRS and the Federal Reserve.

Corrupt Federal Reserve - Robbing Americans Since 1913

http://www.youtube.com/watch?v=BPU8w7Bxc0A

http://www.youtube.com/watch?v=hQZ56hkKOlk

http://www.youtube.com/watch?v=yrGNNZnz8El

The fight to restore our country to Constitutionally protected freedom has been going on for a long time. This old cartoon explains one of the biggest problems facing the nation and the world.

Fredrick Hayek, The Illustrated Road to Serfdom

http://www.mises.org/books/TRTS/

Another classic published in 1950 attempting to wake people up about how our freedom is being lost. Read more about "The Road to Serfdom"

http://en.wikipedia.org/wiki/The_Road_to_Serfdom

New American Century

www.newamericancentury.org

www.newamericancentury.org/RebuildingAmericasDefenses.pdf

George Bush and the other Neocons told the world exactly what their plans were regarding Iraq, Iran, Afghanistan and the entire world before the attacks on 9/11/2001. Read the section describing how another "Pearl Harbor" is needed to motivate the nation.

North American Union Super Highway

www.ciscoport.com

www.canamex.org

www.nascocorridor.com

Ron Paul and his well informed supporters are often ridiculed as being a crazed conspiracy theorist. The plans for a super corridor running through the United States connecting Mexico and Canada are right on the Internet for anyone to see. Look at how the freight will come from China, be inspected in Mexico and travel all the way through the USA to Canada without any approval or oversight by United States Authorities.

Constitution Class 1 of 7, for Patriots of USA Republic

Libertarian Presidential candidate Michael Badnarik teaches an excellent class about the real Constitution of USA

1.   http://video.google.com/videoplay?docid=8321747074978323622
2.   http://video.google.com/videoplay?docid=4870224407360952135
3.   http://video.google.com/videoplay?docid=-8018874590848634400
4.   http://video.google.com/videoplay?docid=-1980674934527237459
5.   http://video.google.com/videoplay?docid=-5509747643152392910
6.   http://video.google.com/videoplay?docid=-3601271545224839349
7.   http://video.google.com/videoplay?docid=5824859883322263421

Iranian Blowback in 1979 from a Coup in 1953

http://www.youtube.com/watch?v=IdgbOxDX6DE

An analysis of Ron Paul's comment made during the May 15, 2007 presidential debate about "blowback" due to the 1953 Iranian coup. PBS documentary from 1987 explaining the reasons behind the Iranian hostage crisis.

Long Tail

http://www.wired.com/wired/archive/12.10/tail.html

Publisher of Wired Magazine, Cris Anderson, compiled the findings he posted to his long tail blog into a book detailing how lower costs of created by new technology opens up niche markets which combined are greater than the so called mass market.

Kitco

http://www.kitco.com/

Kitco tracks precious metals and currencies

History of Linux Operation System

https://netfiles.uiuc.edu/rhasan/linux/

Linux is the most popular operating system for web servers, the computers that provide all the web sites to you when you surf the world wide web.

Mozilla

https://www.mozilla.org/

The Mozilla suite is free open source software. Its one of the most popular web browsers and leads for features, security and following standards.

Slashdot

http://slashdot.org/

Slashdot is one of the most popular forum sites on the web. So many people read Slashdot that a post there can generate more traffic that a web server can handle. Being overrun with too much traffic is called being "slashdotted".

Sourceforge

http://web.sourceforge.com/

SourceForge is the global technology community's hub for information exchange, open source software distribution and services, and goods for geeks. Most open source projects are managed using Sourceforge.

Digg.com

http://www.digg.com/

Digg is a place for people to discover and share content across the web.. Digg surfaces the best stuff as voted on by our users.

Predictive Innovation

http://www.MarkProffitt.com

The Predictive Innovation Method makes it possible to stay ahead of global competition in the quickly changing distributed environment.

Federal Reserve Says USA is Upside Down on Debt

http://www.iht.com/articles/ap/2008/03/06/business/NA-FIN-ECO-US-Home-Equity.php

Homeowners owe more on mortgages than their houses are worth.

Epilogue

In January 2008 a delegation of over 20 prominent Ron Paul supporters demanded changes in the way the national campaign was being run. The official campaign completely mishandled several issues including claims of racism and abandoned the Michigan campaign. Those two items alone were probably enough to ruin his chances of winning. He could have swept the primary in Michigan because the Democratic National Committee nullified their primary so all the Democrats could have voted for Ron Paul without any effect on the Democratic race.

Many people spent fortunes and even quit their jobs to work for free to get Ron Paul elected. One supporter spent $250,000 of his own money to run full page ads in the USA Today. Another had forgone $60,000 income and mortgaged his house to dedicate himself full time to the campaign.

The delegation located experts who had been responsible for winning three presidential elections in Europe. The delegation of supporters flew to Texas to present a signed statement of their requests. Ron Paul received the statement but failed to act on it. The experts were never contacted and only a couple cosmetic changes occurred in the campaign. That spelled the doom of Ron Paul for President 2008.

Support evaporated after the delegation was rebuffed. When it became clear the professional politicians failed and the grassroots was responsible for all the success, the official campaign started implementing more of the items on the list. It was too late.

As principled and dedicated as Ron Paul is, he is not the solution for the problems facing the USA and the world. No single person can give you freedom. You must choose to be free and act on your choice. Centralized organization can't understand and deal with the distributed nature of freedom. Centralized organizations can never move as quickly or have as much or as accurate information as a highly connected distributed group of individuals. The weight of bureaucracy, even when headed by a benevolent leader will doom it to failure.

The Ron Paul Revolution of 2007 woke up millions of people around the world to the coming downfall of the old centralized command and control thinking. These people know what to watch for as events unfold.

The financial crisis continues to grow and everything Ron Paul warned came true. On March 6, 2008 the Federal Reserve announced homeowners equity was bellow 50%. That means the combine value of all the houses in the USA is less than the total amount owed. Hopefully it will be remembered that Ron Paul warned of this and offered the solution.

Despite all the negative events I hope people will not get disillusioned. I hope they see what they actually accomplished. They succeeded. This book is one more attempt to motivate people around the world to look past government, embrace freedom, and enjoy the rewards it provides.

We are at a turning point. The transition will be difficult for many people. Learning new skills to function in the changing world will be essential. I will continue writing books, speaking and posting information on my blog, www.MarkProffitt.com, to help people learn how they can build the wonderful future that is possible.

Illustration Index

Alphabetical Index